PRIVATEE

MW01295661

Bank of Crooks & Criminals

How a banker robbed a customer at the point of a pen

KEN ROSSIGNOL

News and Commentary

News & Commentary

The views and commentary associated with this story are the opinions of the author based on the evidence presented herein. The reader should feel free to draw any conclusion they wish.

Full disclosure:

The author has a banking relationship with the Old Line Bank with a mortgage on real estate. The author has agreed to provide consulting and publicity services to Chuck Kimball as of March 1, 2013 to tell the world about his plight as he fights to have his property restored to him or be compensated by Old Line Bank.

Charles S. "Chuck" Kimball seated on the porch of one of his suites at River Creek Lodge, St. George Island, Maryland, and with his son, Bipper, looking out over the Potomac

Bank of Crooks & Criminals

River.

KEN ROSSIGNOL

Chapter One

With the Great Recession which got underway in 2006, came plenty of trouble for the nation's economy as many people lost their homes and businesses to the ravages of economic downturn through foreclosure. This story is about a man who lost everything, not due to the economy but due to the scheming and fraudulent acts of his bank.

Charles "Chuck" Kimball had been selling land and building homes for forty years when he finished his latest projects at the sites of historic old hotels on waterfront locations in St. Mary's County, Maryland when a new opportunity came available. Kimball, who served in the Marines as a young man, was adept at taking distressed and undervalued properties along the Maryland shoreline and building new single family and duplex housing. In addition, he was able to successfully develop a large waterfront development after buying the property from a federal agency which wound up with the land, the Resolution Trust Corporation, following a major banking scandal. Kimball had also began a floating development of houseboats which ground to a halt with opposition coming from neighbors who wished to keep their vistas to themselves and not share them with a marina full of floating homes.

Kimball never lacked for imagination and his wife July worked alongside him in renovating, painting and decorating existing properties and in designing new ones. Kimball razed a waterfront mobile home park and replaced it with a community of pricey waterfront duplexes at Piney Point, Maryland. The old Oakwood

Lodge was flooded and blown apart during Hurricane Isabel in 2003 and also soon became a new condo project of waterfront pricey homes built from the ground up by Kimball to replace the decades-old lodge.

The day Kimball was signing the contract for the once-bustling Swann's Pier, the old hotel burned to the ground, speeding up the planned removal and replacement with a dozen duplexes, offering unique views of sunrises and sunsets from each home.

When Bill Blanton, who owned the Evans Seafood restaurant, a famous local crabhouse on St. George Island told Kimball he was ready to sell, Kimball began to get his mind whirring with ideas on what to do with the once-bustling crabhouse. Evans enjoyed such a great reputation that most people planned ahead on waiting more than an hour to get in the front door and did so without complaint. The parking lot would be overflowing with vehicles and those in line would spend time in the bar which had been added on the front of the busy place. Evans was so busy that it only closed up one day a week and finally would shut down for a month after the Christmas parties were over, so the big family of Robert "Bugs" Evans could take a break.

Bugs acted as the host and seated people, kept track of orders and often were the cashier as well, with his children taking over most of the key roles in the place as he and his wife aged. The Evans family served what they caught in the Potomac and bought fresh fish and crabs from scores of local watermen as well, earning the establishment a reputation as having fresh-caught and well-prepared local seafood. There weren't any fancy French names for entrees or silly ways to cook crabs, fish and oysters perpetrated upon their customers. There were experienced country-folks who

KEN ROSSIGNOL

knew how to cook local seafood in the kitchen, which is all that matters in a crabhouse.

Joining a large group at the old Evans for dinner one night, for the first time, one customer was up to his elbows in crabs served on the brown paper spread across the table when the waitress said she had to clear up the mess. The customer protested and said he could still eat a bunch more crabs. The woman said she was going to bring out dinner; the man was stunned and said that he thought the crabs were dinner. The woman laughed and said, 'honey, you ain't seen nothing yet'. She was right, as the group was getting the Evans Special, all-you-can-eat, family style, and platters of fried oysters, fish, clams, crab balls and hushpuppies began to appear, with each refilled every time they were emptied. Homemade cole slaw and oyster stew filled out the offerings as pitchers of beer were constantly brought to the tableside.

Chuck Kimball, with his lodge in the background.

Chapter Two

In 2004, Bill Blanton, who had bought the property from the Evans family, and Kimball agreed on a price and transferred ownership to Kimball, who immediately began to plan his changes which included building a three-story lodge and construction of a new restaurant building.

The existing crabhouse had been expanded to include a second-story which offered wide vistas over St. George Creek to the east and the wide expanse of the Potomac River to the west as the property sat aside a narrow strip of the island. Hurricane Isabel had wreaked havoc on the building in 2003 and it was time for it to be replaced.

Kimball leased the restaurant for a time and then was able to accumulate the permits he needed to bring about his planned construction.

After five years of owning the old Evans Seafood, Chuck Kimball donated the old building to the Second District Volunteer Fire Department to burn as a training exercise. Kimball moved his plans through the St. Mary's County permits office, and in the fall of 2008, was ready to start construction on a new three- story hotel and an attractive restaurant and bar on St. George's Island.

By the spring of 2009, Kimball was opening his new facility, and it looked like a million dollars. Actually it was well over six million. At this point, he needed to finalize his loans for the project as some costs had exceeded his projections.

Kimball, in a deposition for a civil lawsuit involving the property, stated under oath, that Watts "knowingly altered a personal financial statement to show a value of $13,000,000." Kimball says this figure was created by Watts so he could influence another bank to pick up part of the loan which had exceeded the ability of Maryland Bank to make by itself.

Kimball was a first-rate builder but had no skills in the restaurant business and no family available to help him run the restaurant and hotel, a tragic combination which often puts the owner on the fast-track to financial doom. But Chuck had a close relationship with the son-in-law and son of his late buddy, banker Jack Daugherty, the founder of Maryland Bank & Trust Company. The two heirs to Jack Daugherty, G. Thomas Daugherty and Thomas B. Watts, had taken over operation of the bank after the senior Daugherty died. Kimball also had "an angel," a financial backer who had pledged five valuable waterfront lots he owned at The Landings nearby as collateral for the loan.

This source of private lending, Dr. Ngozika J. Nwaneri, with whom Kimball had been doing business for fifteen years, repeated his desire to provide funds Kimball might need to make his payments on the Lodge and restaurant as winter months approached and sales dipped below the costs of carrying the notes and expenses.

The bank's CEO was Watts, who told Kimball in 2008 he would have the money he needed to build the new hotel and restaurant.

Kimball had been having a few good years in the building business and was able to get his ducks lined up. By May of 2009, he had built the new lodge and restaurant built and open for business. In July Kimball hosted a grand opening in which he invited several hundred persons to sample the food, browse through the lodge and enjoy the first new hotel built on the Potomac River in one hundred and fifty years.

Chapter Three

Within six months of opening for business, the customers were not coming to the facility at St. George Island in sufficient volume for Kimball to turn a profit, a very typical situation for any new business; made all the more difficult by the Great Recession and the out-of the-way location of the new River-Creek Lodge and Restaurant.

In the hey-day of Bugs Evans, the late owner of the once popular crabhouse, a visit on a typical Sunday afternoon after church would have meant waiting in line in spite of the island being a million miles from anywhere. On weekends city residents from the Washington area would trek down to St. George Island to soak up the view and enjoy the fare, but now, with the economy and a myriad of choices available, the traffic in the restaurant was slow.

By the fall of 2009, the place was often empty while Kimball began to work the defense contractors in Lexington Park to lease rooms and went from one hotel to another along the strip of Rt. 235 and put out flyers on vehicle windshields at 4 am in order to try to steal some business, sometimes setting off car alarms in the process and earning him nasty notes from the motel managers.

By November of the year in which the business opened, Chuck was still making his payments on time and in full. Kimball contends that he could carry the place for as long as he needed to make it work.

Kimball said he had never missed a payment on his loan to the bank. But Maryland Bank and Trust was nervous about its portfolio of commercial real estate loans, and failure of a loan as big as Kimball's could endanger the bank, according to statements made later by Watts to *ST. MARY'S TODAY*. Dozens-- more than 300 -- banks had failed since the current deep recession had begun.

THE FRAUD

Attorney John Norris III, then in private practice and formerly the St. Mary's County Attorney, now serving as Calvert County Attorney, actively represented Maryland Bank and Trust in its quest to have someone take over the Kimball property on St. George's Island. According to one local business owner, Norris asked him in November of 2009 if he wanted the property for six million dollars. The bank would loan him an extra million to help carry the deal. The businessman said no.

Then, according to Kimball, Watts came to him and told him that he had a person who would lease his place from him, and that he and bank president Tom Daugherty would each put up $15,000 of their own money to cover the mortgage payment for November and proceed to take over the place.

Kimball thought it over and realized that as long as his payments were covered, why not? He wasn't a restaurateur, and this didn't sound like a bad deal.

In fact, Kimball said, Watts told him it wasn't a matter of choice; he either agreed or Watts would immediately foreclose.

Commercial loans are typically written, so that regardless of any of the terms, the lending institution could "call" the loan at any time, giving the borrower few options other than paying off the loan, thus Kimball says that as long as he still owned the property he would bow to Watt's wishes.

Watts told him to be at bank attorney John Norris's office within one hour to sign the lease, or Watts would start foreclosure proceedings that day.

Under direct order from Norris, Kimball says he signed the lease. The lease did not disclose the name of the tenant and Kimball was told a signed copy would be provided to him afterwards.

But Watts told him he had someone to lease the project from him. Kimball says on November 25, 2009, Watts arrived and changed the locks, cleaned out the safe, and told Kimball that Bree Whitlock and a new tenant were going to take over.

THE FACTS

Kimball says he called his attorney, Marc Cohen, who then called Norris and instructed him to not allow Kimball to sign anything until he could get there and review the papers. Kimball says that, once again, Norris told him to sign as soon as he arrived at the law office. He wanted to wait for Cohen, but Norris told him to sign, or the bank would foreclose.

The lease Kimball was told to sign didn't have anyone's name filled in as the person or entity that would be leasing from him.

Kimball's account of that day is supported by a letter written by his attorney, Marc Cohen. Kimball was under duress but, according to him, he repeatedly represents *he never missed a payment*. Yet one morning before he arrived at the Island Inn, Kimball says his business was entered, the money taken from his safe, the locks changed, and not a single court order had authorized the act.

Cohen protested to Norris about having violated his instructions in forcing Kimball to sign the blank lease and told Kimball that he could have Norris disbarred for his actions.

THE FRAUD
Breaking and Entering by Banker

KEN ROSSIGNOL

On Nov. 24, 2009, following the illegal breaking and entering of the property, allegedly by Watts and his new manager, Bree Whitlock, Cohen sent this letter via email to John Norris, with a copy to Kimball:

"I am becoming confused. When I first spoke to you I said the leases were not adequate for Chuck's needs and you said you would be willing to negotiate them to his satisfaction. The next day Tom Watts called Kimball and said he needed something immediately. The next day, Friday morning, he called me and said he absolutely needed something for the auditors on Monday or everything would fall apart. I said I could not draft and negotiate the leases on a few hours' notice but would give him a License would promise a forthcoming lease. He said he was satisfied and I sent it to you and to him.

"Chuck went to your office to sign the License and instead was prevailed upon to sign the two leases which we had discussed were unacceptable and would not work either party.

"He was also asked to sign an affidavit regarding his relations with Watts and Nwaneri which is not entirely accurate and a Resolution and an Assignment assigning away his interest in Potomac Land Ltd., to an unnamed purchaser for an unstated price. Finally, he was presented with and executed the License which is inconsistent with every other document he was asked to sign. He was not given counter-signed documents for any of the foregoing and we have no idea who the license manager or members are.

"Bree started Friday running the place presumably as the licensee and someone changed the locks without authority. Someone also took over the cash and inventory on hand.

What is going on?"
Marc Cohen

The abrupt takeover of the restaurant and lodge took place without a legal lease or any type of written authorization. According to Kimball and documents available, including the reference above, the takeover was a criminal act. A law enforcement official contacted for comment said that the statute of limitations has not run out on this alleged act and those involved could be charged with grand theft and burglary.

THE FACTS

Kimball said that Thomas Watts and Bree Whitlock were the two people involved, that they entered his premises without his permission, changed the locks, that they cleaned out his cash registers, opened and removed money from his office safe, took over his inventory of food and liquor and emptied his bank account of funds which had been processed from credit card charge transactions in the days prior to this event.

Kimball still didn't have a signed copy of the lease, which Watts said had been negotiated with the grandfather of Bree Whitlock, a former employee of Kimball. At this point, his building and contents were taken from him; he had no signed lease and *had never missed a mortgage payment.*

In the HBO hit series *The Sopranos*, all of this would have happened in addition to Kimball being taken out on a boat in the Bay and never seen again. But that's about the only part of *The Sopranos* that was missing from the saga of Maryland Bank and the takeover of Chuck Kimball's Island Inn.

This alleged act of misconduct alone could result in Norris being disbarred according to an expert in rules for attorney conduct. Kimball's attorney, Marc Cohen, was kind enough to have supported Kimball's story with a written reference to that allegation, a copy of which is among all pertinent documents of the affair which

KEN ROSSIGNOL

Kimball received in response to his complaint to the Maryland Attorney Grievance Commission.

Cohen revealed his opinion of the competence of the person Watts installed as the manager of the Kimball property.

In an email to Norris on December 1, 2009, Cohen wrote the following:

"John; It seems to be that we are best served by some informality at this time. I therefore am responding to you in this simple email format.

First, Chuck has been entirely compliant with the MBT directions and wishes. He did not put his company in bankruptcy try to reorganize or to dispose of any company assets to help continue financing the business. Instead, as counseled, he agreed to lease it to a friend of Tom Watts, a fine woman, who has little experience and no demonstrable means to make the lease payments. He has also let her commence operation using his stock-in-trade. In return for this risk and cooperation, he wants a release on all personal liability on the MBT note.

Second, Tom Watts advised Chuck that he would pay the legal expense for this transaction and you could represent both MBT and Chuck and his company since everybody wanted the same thing. He met with you and Tom together and separately to reach an acceptable agreement. However, it is apparent from the documents he signed that everybody clearly did not want the same things. Some of the problems with the documents were fundamental, such as a rent that did not even approximate the carrying costs. Other issues were just the usual drafting effort to give one party more favorable terms and advantages than the other. Accordingly, going forward Chuck will need independent counsel (and as things stand now he has no cash flow to pay for such help.) I will therefore expect either the lease agreements or a separate note from Tom committing to pay my fees. Currently, my bill is modest and if we move forward amicably and expeditiously I presume it will remain so.

Last, the few lease changes needed are not at all dramatic, but will still be adequate to show an arms-length negotiation. However, I would like to confirm that the first two elements discussed above are acceptable to your client before we attempt to finalize the desired leases. If we cannot reach an agreement on the terms set forth above, I will for reasons we have discussed, refer Chuck to other counsel. Marc"

THE FRAUD
On December 7, 2009, Norris sent this email to Cohen:

"Marc; Chuck called me moments ago. I asked that if he is represented by counsel that he speak with that attorney and that I could not speak with him without that attorney's consent. Chuck mentioned your name. So you are aware, drafts amending the Minimum Annual Rent for each the Hotel and Restaurant and ratifying the Leases have been prepared. I didn't want you to work on something that was already done in the event you are still involved. I copied Bipper in the event you are not. Thanks, John"

Watts and Norris ordered Kimball to sign blank leases or face foreclosure, and then Norris created a "phantom corporation" to take over the property. Watts had a personal relationship with Bree Whitlock which may have colored his comprehension of having an unqualified person operate the business.

THE FACTS
On Nov. 24, 2009, Watts and Norris had Kimball sign blank leases and failed to give him copies. On Dec. 7, 2009, Norris refers to the new leases he has drafted.

KEN ROSSIGNOL

By Feb. 10, 2010, attorney Walter Sawyer is claiming the mortgage was two months in arrears, which it was not, and announcing a foreclosure on the property.

Cohen knew Whitlock wasn't capable of running the business for Kimball and didn't act to protect Kimball. Cohen continually took steps to give a vigorous representation for Kimball, which show in the trail of the blizzard of paperwork generated by this saga. His failure to act on Kimball's behalf as aggressively as possible was in part due to Kimball's refusal to file bankruptcy.

It is understandable for Kimball to not want to bankrupt his companies and seek court protection as the bank was warning it would also take his house and leave Chuck and July Kimball on the street. At least Kimball was hoping to walk away with his house, which Cohen apparently was able to skillfully negotiate, which balances some of his other failures as Kimball's attorney.

This article appeared in *ST. MARY'S TODAY* in the January 3rd, 2010 edition.

When an Angel Needs an Angel

ST. GEORGE ISLAND --- It was just four years ago when a Hollywood woman, who is a double amputee, got one of those too good to be true messages that she had won $5,500 and the enclosed cashier's check was the result of winning a foreign lottery. She ran to the bank and deposited the check and then began to pay bills and do some shopping.

It was 'too good to be true' and the bank, formerly known as Mercantile but now part of PNC Bank, told her, two weeks after the fact, that the check was phony and she was liable to the bank for all of the money. In fact, the bank boosted her checking account for her monthly disability check and cleaned her out. She was given notice that she would be paying the bank back for a long time.

A local builder learned of the woman's misfortune and he had just had a good year. Just prior to Christmas, this builder, Chuck Kimball, went and visited the woman and gave her $1,000 out of his pocket. In addition, he went to the bank, which at that time still had a figurehead president in residence in Leonardtown. The builder gave a convincing request to the banker to write off the rest of the loss, $3,500, which was actually caused by them. As part of Kimball's deal with the bank, he donated another $1,000 out of his pocket to the 2nd District Volunteer Fire and Rescue of Valley Lee.

The bank had a responsibility to its customers to warn them of such bank check fraud, an action that most banks take very seriously and use electronic and written warning notices as well as post signs at teller booths. But Mercantile, now PNC, had taken no such action and when the cashier's check came in from a bank in a foreign country, the funds were immediately made available. Anyone trying to deposit a check of any significance in recent years knows that their bank will put a hold on the funds and deny availability for up to two weeks while the check clears.

But no one at the bank helped Connie Hewlett until Chuck Kimball came along.

Hewlett, who has artificial feet, stands on her own with braces and she has been standing on her own two feet for a long time. But she was defeated and despondent until Chuck Kimball decided to be her angel.

Kimball knows a thing or two about angels.

As a land developer, Kimball has been up and down and all around. Like the old Sinatra song, he has been a pauper, a pirate, a poet and a king. He says he knows

... *"what it is like to poor and what it is like to be on top, and boy, is being on top better!"*

But now Chuck needs an angel.

After years of land speculation, buying several marinas, a couple of times, selling C-Hawk boats with a flair for matching folks up to quality power boats, building houseboats until he was driven out of business by environmentalists who didn't want people living in houseboats; putting together a land scheme which faltered; went broke and then was able to buy back the same project from the government agency which wound up with it after the bank went busted; Kimball has gone through nine lives and run out of feet to land on.

Kimball has built the nicest waterfront home project in the area at the Landings at Piney Point. That is the project he was able to conjure up in the late seventies when no one thought it was possible, saw it go bust in the eighties, come to fruition in the nineties and just last year Kimball remembered his late friend and banker Jack Daugherty's phone call with the receiver for the federal agency trying to sell the unfinished development. Daugherty wrote Kimball a personal check for a million dollars and guaranteed the funds for the check for Kimball in that call. Finally, The Landings was complete.

Kimball cruised into the twenty-first century with the optimism and vitality of the entrepreneur who made America great.

As the first few years of the first decade of this century began, Kimball saw opportunity where others saw decay and neglect. He bought the old Swann's Pier and Oakwood Lodge properties, turned them both into bonfires and in their places, built new and desirable waterfront properties. The old trailer park at Piney Point caught Chuck's eye about ten years ago and he went into that property and churned it into new salt box *style duplexes, all with water views, access to the beach and oriented to the water.*

What had been a troubled part of the Piney Point community became an asset and boosted local tax collections as families quickly bought all of the homes.

Kimball always made his adventures a family affair. His two sons were mechanics, boat salesmen, carpenters, and eventually construction managers. His wife July was the designer, office staff and executive sales coordinator. When Chuck Kimball would romance a buyer with grand vistas of fun and frolic on the riverfront, his family went to work to make his visions come true for everyone. Kimball knew he had married up and July provided grace and style to Chuck's bluster and bulldog persona.

When Kimball applied for a bank loan he suddenly discovered that the Federal Government had declared his wife dead, with a payout for a grave marker having been made. Kimball thanks Congressman Steny Hoyer for bringing his bride back from the dead, when John Bohanan was able to convince the government it had made an error and the notation on Kimball's credit report was corrected to show July alive and well.

Not long ago, Kimball showed that his visionary talent was still alive. He viewed a new Evans Seafood at St. George Island, complete with a lodge for visitors to stay, a pier to host a fleet of charter boats and all of it built above the flood levels of visiting hurricanes.

Many hurdles were crossed as Kimball figured he would have one big last accomplishment in his long life. The barrel-chested Marine worked long and hard to gather permits, appear at hearings, pay engineers and attorneys, finagle bank loans, schmooze land use officials, capture the imagination of the neighbors on the island and finally, after several years, got his permits.

Evans was finished and some months later, the lodge was done and all open to the public.

The River Creek Lodge was the first and only new hotel to be built on the Potomac River south of Washington in more than 150 years.

But by the time the reality of all this came to pass, the United States and the rest of the world plunged into a depression, deep and dark and dangerous.

Kimball's options of selling the lodge and restaurant to an operator got caught up in the inability of buyers to obtain loans as banks tightened credit, despite the bailouts designed to encourage lending.

The financial reality of servicing monthly mortgage payments arrived as revenue was diminished and refinancing made impossible.

At this point, various financial arrangements are being sought by Kimball with his bank but his home is listed for sale, which sure isn't a good sign. Chuck Kimball had to pledge his home to get his financing, showing his commitment to his final development.

Chuck Kimball is a product of American ingenuity and has left a trail of responsible developments, quality construction and gained hundreds of friends and admirers in the process. He has made St. Mary's County an immeasurably better place, replacing worn out and tired old structures with new homes. He brought to life an old farm on the water next to the oil tank farm and convinced folks to buy impressive big homes. Kimball improved the tax base incredibly with his work.

Kimball may lose everything and if he does, he won't be the only one that loses. We all lose when the brave and the spirited are beaten.

Angels have visited Chuck Kimball before and just four years ago, Chuck Kimball made the bell ring for Connie Hewlett. Connie will tell you she believes in Angels.

Time will tell if an Angel appears again for Chuck and helps him find a way to keep his dream alive.

THE FACTS

Watts asserted in a phone conversation, following the news article that appeared in January of 2010 in *St. Mary's Today,* that he had to take over Kimball's business. Watts said that business was picking up at the Island Inn and Bar, and that they had a good New Year's Eve, with St. Mary's County Commissioner President Jack Russell and other guests packing the place. Watts personally negotiated the cost and placed ads in the *St. Mary's Today* newspaper promoting the changes at the Island Bar and Grill. The ads ran weekly for six months. These efforts on Watt's part indicate that he and the bank were the owners and operators of the LLC which had been formed by attorney John Norris and had seized control of Kimball's business and property.

Kimball was in Florida when he first learned of the bank's decision to foreclose on his property and that an ad had appeared in *The Enterprise* advertising the pending foreclosure. When contacted about the distress of his business, Kimball was optimistic that he would work out his financial affairs, and said that he had a gag order on him and really couldn't talk about his situation.

The front page article in *St. Mary's Today* described what the public could see: Kimball was out of the Island Inn, and someone else was in it and running it for the bank. The article scanned the years of Kimball's construction and redevelopment business and told of his generosity several years before in coming to the aid

KEN ROSSIGNOL

of a Hollywood woman who had her bank account wiped out by Mercantile Bank.

Kimball said Watts was furious about the *St. Mary's Today* article and said that the entire affair could sink the bank.

THE FRAUD

Maryland Bank foreclosed on Kimball's business on February 26, 2010, and he was able to sell his house and make a little money. After Kimball signed a lengthy statement prepared by Watts, the bank released Kimball's house from the loan for the Inn.

But Kimball was, and is, down for the count. He lost $4 million on the Island Inn deal, and the bank ended up with his property.

And he never missed a payment.

A Bank Lawyer's View

On February 4, 2010, Maryland Bank attorney Walter Sawyer wrote to Kimball and advised him that he represented the Maryland Bank & Trust Co. and began to describe the property as being beautiful and scenic, the Lodge as having water views for all rooms and "are the best in Southern Maryland."

Clearly any failure to have the hotel packed with customers must have been Kimball's fault, according to the tone of Sawyer's letter.

Then Sawyer proceeded to assign blame.
"Unfortunately, there were significant cost overruns in the construction of the Lodge. It was anticipated that the Lodge could generate more than enough income to make the mortgage payments. Unfortunately, after the Lodge opened, the occupancy rate has been so low, that the income generated by the business has not been able to pay the expenses with no ability to make any mortgage payments whatsoever."

Sawyer's letter ignored the fact that the "cost over-runs" had been covered by the financial backer of

2º

Bank of Crooks & Criminals

Kimball and sufficient funds and properties had been posted as collateral to cover those cost over-runs. Sawyer then went on to state the terms of the Indemnity Deed of Trust which delineated how and what cures were available to the Bank.

"In your case, the only way you were able to make the mortgage payments were from your own funds. You have exhausted your funds. You or your various entities no longer have the ability to make this payment. Further, your projection concerning the income generated from this project has not been met, and this fact has seriously affected the value of this real estate."

Again, Sawyer ignored the fact that he and Norris had withheld from Kimball the "phantom lease" for his property, which assigned the responsibility for making the mortgage payments to Watts and the bank.

At this point in his letter, Sawyer may have become part of a criminal conspiracy to defraud.

"I have reviewed the profit and loss statements from the business, and one can only conclude that it is impossible for anyone to make the mortgage payments from the income generated. In fact it appears that in most months there was a loss even without the mortgage payment. Since September 2009, the income has been steadily decreasing. Your tenant made two (2) mortgage payments and has no more funds to make the mortgage payments. This should not surprise you. The December 30, 2009 and January 20, 2010 payment has not yet been paid and the mortgage arrearages are now $66,496.48. Now we are in the winter months, and the financial position continues to decline. I would also note that the hazard insurance and flood insurance has been cancelled, and the county and state real estate taxes have not been paid..."

THE FRAUD

After reciting that his client, the bank, "is attempting to continue to operate the business, with the hope of finding a buyer," Sawyer noted that the bank would have to keep feeding "substantial funds" to "keep the doors open."

And of course, this was all Kimball's fault, according to Sawyer's letter.

THE FACTS

In this letter, Sawyer referred to the "tenant" and said the tenant had no more funds. However, Sawyer did not admit that the tenant was in fact Watts and the bank, which he now states were faced with having to feed substantial funds into the business.

Talk about having it both ways!

Watts and Maryland Bank, under threat of foreclosure and with attorney John Norris doing their bidding, forced Kimball into signing a blank lease and handing over his business to a "ghost tenant," who actually was the bank, and then blamed Kimball for the business failing. Sawyer's letter of February 4, 2010, laid out the steps for the foreclosure which took place on February 26, 2010.

Sawyer admitted his complicity in the deal when he said he had *"reviewed the profit and loss statements,"* for if he actually did so, he knew that the "tenant" was really the bank, something that Kimball did not know. Watts had told him that the tenant was Whitlock's grandfather, who owned several strip joints on the infamous "block", the sin center of strip club bars, in Baltimore. Sawyer personally profited from the rush to foreclosure on Kimball. He received a $20,000 "trustee's fee," according to court auditor J. Ernest Bell II. And regardless of what Kimball claims Watts told him, Cohen continued to request copies of the lease from Norris, *who never provided them.* (**AUTHOR'S NOTE**: Should the Attorney Grievance Commission ever wish to investigate this case, *for real*, they might want to check on this item.)

THE FRAUD

As shown by the following email messages from Marc Cohen to John B. Norris III, Cohen was unaware that Maryand Bank & Trust was ready to foreclose on Kimball and violate the agreement that was reached on Dec. 11, 2009. Since the Kimball's had met all of the conditions set forth in the deal which was sought by Thomas B. Watts, Cohen was anxious to get the final papers of that deal, especially the release for the Kimball's and the payment of the fee for his law firm by the Bank, as had been arranged.

On Feb. 8, 2010, Marc K. Cohen sent an email letter to John B. Norris III, requesting that he provide the release for Kimball's house and payment of his fee to his law firm.

"John, I am still waiting for you to complete the three items listed below per my Jan. 21st email to you and follow-up letters. Chuck is feeling very uneasy about MB&T's follow through on these promises. I also stopped by your office as we discussed after court on the 28th to get my binder and was told it was still not ready, but could be ready the next day. That was nearly two weeks ago. Can I come up and get our documents now? Marc."

"John, per language (cited in Letter of Intent of Dec. 11, 2009) MB&T's release is 30 days overdue. Can we get it next week? Also, have you sent invoice to MB&T and completed settlement binders? Appreciate your getting this resolved. Client is a bit agitated. Marc."

Cohen Denies There is Cause to Foreclose

On February 15, 2010, also on Ober/Kaler letterhead, Cohen wrote to Walter Sawyer, an attorney for Maryland Bank and Trust. In that letter, Cohen

KEN ROSSIGNOL

recited the events of November 2009 when Maryland Bank CEO Tom Watts told Kimball that he had a principal who would lease the property from him, that the payments would be made, and that Bree Whitlock would immediately take possession of the property as the operator, as this was the best plan to keep the business out of default.

THE FRAUD

Cohen told Sawyer in the letter that Maryland Bank had not kept its word in providing copies of documents regarding the lease.

"On Dec. 11th, Mr. Kimball and I met with counsel for MB&T and executed a Collateral Release Agreement, Lease Amendments and other documents intended to keep the project solvent and provide Chesapeake (the legal name of Kimball's firm) and Mr. Kimball certain other consideration, including payment of its outstanding attorney fees occasioned by the initial inappropriate executions. MB&T's counsel, following closing, was to provide closing binders to the parties. To date, despite requests, we have not received our binder or copies of the documents. Similarly Mr. Kimball has not received the MB&T release, and it is possible that you have not been provided these documents either.

THE FACTS

"In sum, based on the request of MB&T and its assurances that the leases and other assignments by Mr. Kimball and Chesapeake would provide for meeting their indebtedness and ensure the continued operation of the project, MB&T is owed no arrearages and has no basis to foreclose. Chesapeake and Mr. Kimball intend to continue to meet their obligations to MB&T and its principals, but also expect these parties to follow through with their promises."

In a lengthy series of emails on Dec. 10, 2009, Norris and Cohen sent a series of notes about drafts of a

Bank of Crooks & Criminals

Letter of Intent, to replace the "phantom lease" which
John B. Norris had illegally withheld from both Marc K.
Cohen and Kimball and had been signed by Kimball
under threat of foreclosure —at the order of Norris in
direct contradiction of the orders of Kimball's attorney.

Cohen wrote to Norris:

*"John: The LOI reflects awareness of the stresses
and the rash acts that follow on both sides. The place to
ratify the agreed transactional documents and release
the house is the same agreement. Can you have a draft
tomorrow so we can execute it and the liquor board
form? There is no time or retainer left for any longer
negotiation."*

Norris wrote to Cohen:

*"Marc: I am reviewing your proposed revisions to
the Letter of Intent; thank you for tracking the changes.
In light of the acts renouncing and disavowing the
Assignment of Membership Interests in Chesapeake-
Stafford Restaurants, LLC and renouncing the accuracy
of his affidavit, it would be foolhardy on my part to
recommend signing the Letter of Intent without
resolution of all matters that arose subsequent to Mr.
Kimball signing of these and other documents last week.
Therefore, I request an opinion of counsel confirming
the validity of the Assignment of Membership interest as
a valid and enforceable agreement to transfer those
interests to a trustee, or a properly executed, revised
Assignment accomplishing the same effect and either
ratification or amendment of Mr. Kimball's affidavit
signed last week. A further issue is the renunciation of
the Leases for the Lodge and Restaurant. To date, we
have received no proposed revision to the Leases.
Unfortunately, the repudiation of the acts I reasonably
believed Mr. Kimball took knowingly and willingly have
caused an erosion of trust; that in my opinion, requires*

KEN ROSSIGNOL

the entirety of all issues be bundled. Therefore, please advise if all of the foregoing, including the Leases, the Affidavit and the Assignment, are intended to be addressed concurrently or if the sole presentation on behalf of Mr. Kimball is the proposed revisions to the Letter of Intent you submitted earlier today. Thank you, John."

THE FRAUD

Kimball claims that "none of the above is true" and that Norris had called him and instructed him not to send a copy of the Affidavit, which purported to show, falsely, that Dr. Nwaneri was a business partner to Kimball in the River Creek Lodge business. Kimball reiterated that Norris still had not provided a copy of the lease he was forced to sign and failed to return calls requesting the copies.

On December 11, 2009, the Letter of Intent was signed by Watts and the Kimball's.

Marked "confidential" the document prohibited disclosure of the terms except for legally required purposes, such as Mrs. Nwaneri filing civil suit against Old Line Bank. As part of those proceedings, Kimball was ordered to bring any and all documents pertaining to the transaction and loan with Maryland Bank and make them part of the record.

The Letter of Intent is prepared and signed by Watts and addressed to July and Charles Kimball.

"As you recall, you each personally guaranteed a loan from Maryland Bank & Trust Company N. A. and payments upon that loan are current, due to your recent decision to lease the restaurant and Lodge. I understand, though, that you have raised some concern regarding the possible future sale of your home located at 18234 River Road in Tall Timbers, Maryland (the "House"). That property is not currently collateral for the loans guaranteed by each of you jointly and

2 6

Bank of Crooks & Criminals

severally. In accordance with our recent discussion, I am
offering this Letter of Intent for your countersignature
that, upon satisfaction of certain conditions, I will
execute appropriate documents to confirm a release of
any proceeds from the sale of the House by and on
behalf of Maryland Bank & Trust Company, N.A. This
letter sets forth the conditions precedent and
conditions subsequent affecting the voluntary
obligation I am proffering in consideration of your full
and complete satisfaction of these conditions. Please
have your attorney review these terms and if
acceptable, countersign one original and return it to my
attorney's office at P. O. Box 858, Leonardtown,
Maryland 20650.

"I believe that we all recognize that there may be
synergies between the restaurant and hotel built by
Potomac Land Ltd., and those synergies as well as the
individual strengths of each asset must be managed in a
manner to maximize the return of investment income.
Presently, Chesapeake Stafford Restaurants LLC, a
Virginia limited liability company whose membership
interests are wholly held by Potomac Land Ltd., has
relet the properties located at 16800 Piney Point Rd.,
and 16810 Piney Point Rd.,(hereinafter, collectively
referred to as the "Properties", improvements thereon
and personal property therein to Island Dining, LLC and
Island Hospitality, LLC. Based upon your representations
of your current finances, the potential for repayment of
the loan made by Maryland Bank & Trust Company,
N.A. largely, if not wholly, depends upon the successful
generation of income by the operations of the
Properties. My experience tells me that profits most
closely follow cooperation by and between Chesapeake
Stafford Restaurants, Potomac Land Ltd., yourselves,
and Island Dining, LLC and Island Hospitality, LLC. In

KEN ROSSIGNOL

order to induce that cooperative effort, I offer the execution of any documents by and on behalf of Maryland Bank & Trust Company, N. A. that effectuate a release of the premises located at 18237 River Road in Tall Timbers Maryland for no additional consideration upon satisfaction of the following conditions precedent, which shall remain valid and enforceable so long as the following conditions subsequent are met.

Conditions Precedent:

1. This binding letter of intent and such papers as required by the liquor board for the permission to use the liquor license at the Properties shall be exchanged by close of business on December 11, 2009.
2. Charles Kimball shall provide all current passwords, password reset keys, program disks, manuals and product keys for computer programs used in the businesses located upon the Properties.
3. Charles Kimball shall provide the combination to all safes and safety deposit boxes located upon the premises.
4. Charles Kimball shall provide the passwords for all equipment requiring a password and located or used upon the Properties.
5. Charles and July Kimball shall cooperate with the owners and representatives of Island Dining, LLC and Island Hospitality, LLC and not interfere with operations conducted upon the Properties.

"As mentioned above, on or about December 18, 2009, subject to satisfactory completion of the foregoing, I will execute on behalf of Maryland Bank & Trust Company, N.A. any and all documents that effectuate a release of the House and the proceeds from the sale of the House for no additional consideration, which shall remain valid and enforceable subject to the following conditions subsequent, whereupon the material failure of any one of the conditions subsequent is deemed a material breach of this agreement and shall operate to invalidate such documents.

Conditions Subsequent:

1. Charles and July Kimball shall cooperate with the owners and representatives of Island Dining, LLC and Island Hospitality, LLC and provide any additional information or thing necessary or proper for the operations conducted upon the Properties to the extent they have access to the foregoing.

2. 2. Charles Kimball shall provide, within fifteen (15) days of his signature upon this document all drawings, sketches, plans, permits, applications, approvals, certificates of occupancy, construction drawings, site plans (including, without limitation, plans for the yet-unconstructed waterfront deck), releases of liens, proofs of purchase and payment in full, warranties and all other documents related to the construction of improvements upon the Properties, and personally located upon the Properties in whatever form he has or has access to the foregoing.

3. For a period of Ninety (90) days following full execution of this agreement Charles and July Kimball shall cooperate and not directly or indirectly interfere with the operations located upon the Premises.

4. Charles and July Kimball shall not enter upon the Properties except as paying guests of the operations conducted upon the Properties or

KEN ROSSIGNOL

at the invitation or request of myself or a
member of Island Hospitality, LLC or Island
Dining, LLC.

5. When upon the Properties, neither Charles or
July Kimball shall act in any manner other than
cordial and personable with any member of
Island Hospitality, LLC or Island Dining, LLC, any
member of the staff of the businesses
conducted upon the properties, and any guest
or business invitee located upon the
Properties.

6. Neither Charles nor July Kimball shall discuss
the businesses conducted upon the properties
except in a manner that is positive and reflects
sincere best wishes for the success of the
businesses and all persons involved in said
businesses.

7. Charles Kimball shall execute and deliver all
documents necessary to assign the right to use
the liquor license and Charles and July Kimball
shall fully cooperate and support the
application for a new liquor license upon the
Properties.

8. This Letter of Intent shall remain confidential
and not be disclose, nor the existence of this
Letter of Intent or resulting documents to any
other person by either July or Charles Kimball,
without my prior written permission or as
required by law.

9. Any and all documents I will execute evidencing
a release of the premises located at 18234
River Road in Tall Timbers, Maryland shall
remain confidential and not be disclosed, nor
the existence of such documents be disclosed
to any other person by either Charles or July

> Kimball without my prior permission or as required by law.

10. Charles and July Kimball shall hold harmless and indemnify me and my agents against every and all costs, damages and expenses of whatever kind and in every nature that arises from or is related to a breach of any condition of this agreement.

All cooperation by Charles and July Kimball shall be reasonable, truthful and in good faith but without expenditure of money by them.

In order to evidence your concurrence, I would appreciate your executing and returning a copy of this letter which has been enclosed for that purpose. By signing, you acknowledge that, except for the terms and conditions expressly enumerated in this Agreement, none of the undersigned has made any promises, warranties or representations to any other parties hereto that concern any aspect of the settlement of the matters referred to in this Letter of Intent and that any such promises, warranties or representations which may have been alleged to have been made, are merged herein. You are also acknowledging that this Letter of Intent shall be construed without regard to any presumption requiring construction against the party causing the Letter of Intent to be drafted. Signing this Letter of Intent by us shall constitute approval and acceptance of the principal terms stated herein. It is understood that this Letter of Intent is intended to constitute a legally binding obligation of all parties hereto and their respective heirs, personal and legal representatives, successors, assigns, attorneys and agents. Therefore, please seek the advice of your counsel, if any, prior to countersigning and returning a copy of this Letter of Intent. I remain, very truly yours,

KEN ROSSIGNOL
Thomas Watts."

Chapter Four

The Old Line Bank, which bailed out Maryland Bank & Trust, entered into a deal in 2011 with hotel operator Tommy Waring's Cherry Cove Hospitality to operate the Kimball property. Waring is a successful businessman with half a dozen hotels in Southern Maryland and has a significant staff. It appears now, in 2013, that a new firm has taken over from Waring's company, which failed to make a go of the operation.

Reviews of the restaurant and lodge on Trip Advisor, a web-based travel guide, during the time period that the lessee chosen by the bank after the ouster of Kimball, are mixed with some posting that they loved the views and vistas of the Lodge while others reported on being bumped from their booked rooms without cause or notice only to be sent to another one of the company's hotels in Lexington Park; filthy rooms, noise through the walls, signs on the pier warning against fishing or crabbing (odd for a lodge that promotes same as a reason for staying there), cockroaches, flies, non-existent continental breakfast and awful food in the restaurant operated by Cherry Cove Hospitality.

It remains to be seen if the newest hotel operator can make people believe they have actually arrived at a crab house on St. George's Island if and when it reopens in April, or if they are in just another trendy dining spot that serves frozen food prepared in microwaves. *The proof isn't in the pudding, it's in the crabcakes.*

But while Maryland Bank was in the process of wrapping up the foreclosure on Kimball in early 2010; the bank itself would soon disappear as it was in trouble.

KEN ROSSIGNOL

According to Banktracker.com, an investigative reporting workshop of the American University School of Communication, Maryland Bank was losing money in 2010, and as of March 31, 2011, was still in the red. Its total troubled assets had increased from $14,619,000 to more than $22 million in one year, out of a total of about $350 million in assets.

In comparison, Banktracker.com shows Old Line Bank making a small profit, while its troubled assets were $1.7 million in 2010 and had risen to $3.5 million in 2011. Old Line Bank was of similar size in assets and branches as Maryland Bank & Trust, but is much healthier. Old Line Bank shows no loans which are ninety days or more past due, while Maryland Bank grew from only $10,000 in such loans in 2010 to over $1 million in 2011.

The only other local banks, County First and Community Bank of Tri County, are also rated by Banktracker.com. In 2011, Community Bank had a growing problem with over $22 million in troubled assets, while County First has just over $5 million in troubled assets.

Community Bank received $15,540,000 in Troubled Asset Relief Program TARP funds on December 19, 2008, and apparently has paid the money back after Sept. 30, 2011. There are no local banks now listed as owing TARP money from the bank bailout of 2008. Bank failures are down and bank profits are up, according to Banktracker.com.

By September of 2012, the financial health of Community Bank of Tri-County worsened if one pays attention to the significant increase of troubled assets, which reached $27,606,000. County First had a much smaller increase in its troubled assets to $6,109,000. But Community had a profit of about $3.9 million while County First had reported a profit of only $700,000, which may explain why they do not allow customers to use restrooms in the bank and thereby save on toilet paper. Old Line Bank was continuing to increase its troubled assets to $11.5 million but showed the best profit of all three banks: $5,956,000 as of Sept. 30, 2012.

A once-flourishing operation with ten branches, Maryland Bank & Trust was sold for $20 million in cash and stocks to Old Line Bank. Perhaps appropriately, they consummated the transaction on April Fool's Day, 2011.

THE FRAUD

A joint press release issued by both banks on Sept. 1, 2010, was a spin-doctor's dream, attempting to put a cheerful face on a dire condition. Old Line CEO Cornelsen said that the "acquisition" was a great opportunity for Old Line to increase earnings and generate returns for stockholders of both banks. Watts said that by joining Old Line, they could continue the tradition of the 50-year-old bank of being a Maryland-based community bank. The press release noted that Ober/Kaler was legal counsel for the deal for Old Line Bank.

THE FACTS

Maryland Bank and Trust had been ordered under a strict enforcement action placed on the institution on Feb. 10, 2006 which placed stringent control procedures on the bank, including instructions to *hire competent management,* increase the capitalization and put the bank on the fast track to be closed by the Comptroller of the Currency if need be. Enforcement Action #2006-17 is a public document available to anyone. The thirty page document required the signatures of all members of the Board of Directors.

KEN ROSSIGNOL

To many, the sale of Maryland Bank gave every appearance of being a forced sale designed to save the FDIC from taking over the bank. Nationwide, more than three hundred banks have failed since January 1, 2009, thru Oct. 2011, with even more since then, according to Banktracker.com.

The former branches of Maryland Bank & Trust which were taken over by the Old Line Bank were once bustling with customers and teeming with employees. Now they are staffed with a skeleton crew. Where a large portrait of Jack Daugherty hangs in the lobby of the Lexington Park branch summons a reminder of the days when "Big Daddy Warbucks" popped out of his office in the main lobby to greet customers, there are only two tellers, and there is never a line.

The once elaborate displays of Christmas villages in the bank lobby during the holiday season have vanished as have decorations at the other branches. A teller said that the bank management wanted to present a more professional image but that the change in holiday decorations came from Watts, not from Old Line.

The portrait of bank founder Jack Daugherty in the lobby of the Lexington Park branch is the only reminder of busier days.

THE FRAUD

When the sale of the bank was publicly announced, Kimball tried to get a financial accounting of his transaction from Maryland Bank and Trust, and he claims that all of his requests were refused. Kimball says that he sent certified letters to Old Line Bank who basically told him that they had nothing to do with his troubles.

On January 29, 2011, Kimball sent a letter to Christine Rush, a bank officer with whom he had had an appointment to discuss the liability of Old Line in taking over Maryland Bank. Kimball pointed out that she had agreed to meet with him, and then when he appeared for the meeting, she had informed him that the bank attorney cancelled their meeting.

"If you choose to completely ignore me, I believe you are placing your bank and the stock holders in jeopardy," Kimball wrote in his letter to Rush.

Letter from Old Line Bank attorney Frank Bonaventure, of Ober/Kaler to Kimball

On February 7, 2011, an attorney for Old Line Bank, Frank Bonaventure Jr., wrote to Kimball. Referencing Kimball's letter to Rush, Bonaventure said, *"According to its records, Old Line Bank does not maintain a banking relationship with you, and it is not in a position to discuss any matters related to your banking relationship with another financial institution."*

This was a pretty snooty way for Bonaventure to address a man whom he had been billing for services as the man's attorney just 13 months earlier.

After Ober/Kaler had been dismissed as the attorney for Old Line, the new attorney, Charles Henderson, complied with many of Kimball's requests and provided documents he had been requesting, many of which are cited here.

THE FACTS
Conflict of Interest on part of Ober/Kaler revealed in billing invoice

Bonaventure had another disclosure he should have made to Kimball. Kimball didn't know it, but Old Line Bank's attorney, Bonaventure, was also his attorney.

Marc K. Cohen, who had been representing Kimball in dealing with John Norris, the attorney for Maryland Bank, was a principal in Ober/Kaler PC.

Bonaventure was also a principal and head of Financial Institutions group at the law firm. The firm's

KEN ROSSIGNOL

website touts Bonaventure as being much sought after by the media and frequently quoted by the *Wall Street Journal.*

Bonaventure is one of three attorneys with Ober/Kaler who billed hours to Kimball, as his attorney, on Dec. 10th, 11th, 14th and 29th of 2009.

The billing invoice to Kimball's firm was for 17.10 hours and the "current fees" as of Jan. 20, 2010, totaled $7206.50, a tidy sum for a series of phone calls and conferences to discuss Kimball's business.

12/1/09 Cohen "Review documents; telephone calls with Chuck Kimball; draft and send Mr. Norris settlement terms. 2.30 hours

12/4/09 Bonaventure "Conference with M. Cohen .50 hours

12/4/09 Rafferty "Conference with Marc Cohen regarding developments for issue, restaurant, bank and related parties, begin Mutual Release .30 hours

12/4/09 Rafferty "Revise and send M. Cohen draft Mutual Release" .40 hours.

12/7/09 Cohen "Meeting with Mr. Chuck Kimball and Mr. Bip Kimball discussing alternatives for operating defenses of MBT claims." 1.80 hours

12/9/09 Rafferty "Conference with Marc Cohen regarding Bank claim, possible house exculpation, alternatives .60 hours

12/9/09 Rafferty "Review fax by Banker regarding LOI .40 hours

12/10/09 Cohen "Meeting with Mr. Rafferty; telephone calls with Mr. Chuck Kimball regarding final settlement requirements; work on documents .60 hours

12/10/09 Rafferty "Comments regarding Exemption LOI, Agreement and settlement. .60 hours

F. Thomas Rafferty billed Kimball a half hour on 12/10/09 for "conference with Cohen regarding LOI and facts and response to opposing counsel Norris.

Also on 12/10/09, Rafferty billed forty minutes for "conference with Cohen and reply to Norris regarding additional documents."

On 12/10/09 Rafferty again billed Kimball's firm twenty minutes for "conference with Cohen regarding response of Norris and reply."

It must have been a long day for Rafferty, as also on 12/10/09 he billed Kimball eighty minutes for "Conference with Cohen; review and revise Letter of Intent.

On 12/11/09, Cohen's billing to Kimball was for four and a half hours for "Meeting with Mr. Kimball, related telephone calls; meeting and review documents and execute at Mr. Norris's office; post execution meeting to list and discuss obligations etc."

On 12/11/09 Rafferty was back at work on Kimball's business, charging ten minutes for "Conference with Cohen regarding status and strategy for Kimball-Watts meeting."

On Dec. 14, 2009 Rafferty once again was hard at works for ten minutes and charged for "Read email and reply to Mr. Cohen regarding document cooperation."

On Dec. 29, 2009, Cohen charged Kimball ninety minutes billing time for "Review Licensing agreement transfer; telephone call with Mr. Chuck Kimball and e-mail regarding same to Mr. Norris."

After contacting the Old Line attorney in July 2011, Kimball said Bonaventure told him that he "didn't feel comfortable talking" to him and hung up the phone. What Bonaventure could have told Kimball was that he had a conflict of interest, in that he and his firm had been representing Kimball as Maryland Bank and Trust Company was busy stealing his property in 2009 and now his firm was representing Old Line Bank which

KEN ROSSIGNOL

absorbed MBT and which clearly didn't want to return the property to Kimball.

No kidding.

40

THE FRAUD
Letter between lawyers shows conflict of interest

It is apparent from documents in Kimball's possession that Maryland Bank & Trust paid the legal fee of $5,000 on behalf of Kimball to Cohen, compromising the client-attorney relationship between Kimball and Cohen.

On January 12, 2010, attorney Marc K. Cohen sent this letter to attorney John B. Norris III:

"Dear John; I presume you are settled in after the first of the year. Could you please follow through with getting my bill to Chesapeake Stafford (Kimball's company) to the bank for payment. Your secretary was also going to prepare closing binders. I have not received mine yet, could you check on the status. Last, I did not hear back from you regarding the software transfer (attached) from one of Chuck's companies, the River Creek Lodge, LLC to Bree. I think you should know she wants it assigned to her personally.

As always, should you have any questions or require additional information, please do not hesitate to contact me. Marc K. Cohen"

Sawyer Dangles Fee for Kimball's Lawyer as Inducement for Paperwork

Even after Cohen's letter to Sawyer on February 10, 2010, declaring that there was no cause for a foreclosure, Sawyer sent a letter to Cohen stating what he needed for the foreclosure sale and reminding Cohen that

"I have a check from Maryland Bank & Trust Co. N.A. in the amount of $5,000.00 which will be disbursed after ratification of the foreclosure and the resolution of the personal property. Please advise."

This letter was another smoking gun of the bank's lawyer paying Kimball's lawyer just three days before the foreclosure, in clear violation of ethics rules of the Maryland Bar.

Was Cohen compromised in representing Kimball when he accepted payment from Maryland Bank & Trust? Did he get the promised money? Did he gain the agreement from his client to be paid the money by his client's adversary? The Bar Counsel could ask these questions.

But don't get your knickers in an uproar, as after all, this is Maryland, a state as corrupt as any in the nation.

It is also clear that Cohen's reference to *"inappropriate executions"* is lawyer language for Norris committing an illegal act in forcing Kimball to sign blank documents under threat of foreclosure.

Should John Norris be disbarred for demanding that Kimball sign the "lease" in blank and before his attorney could arrive? Why would John Norris fail to give copies of the executed lease, even though Watts had seized physical control of Kimball's property without any court order?

Is that a bad thing?

The attorney grievance commission may have had a field day with Kimball's complaint as Norris, Sawyer, and Cohen could all be disciplined for their actions in the matter. The firm of Ober/Kaler could be at risk, as one of their attorneys represented the Old Line Bank in refusing to review an illegal and fraudulent foreclosure which had already been well-documented by another of their attorneys.

And to think this law firm's address is in Baltimore and not Philadelphia, which is the proverbial home of crooked lawyers!

42

Bank of Crooks & Criminals

Kimball has filed complaints against each of these attorneys with the Attorney Grievance Commission. An investigation into their conduct could lead to them being exonerated, disciplined, or disbarred.

After a flurry of letters from the AGC to the three attorneys and their responses, the AGC dropped the complaint and so informed Kimball.

Letter in response to Attorney Grievance Commission from Walter W. Sawyer III

Sawyer wrote to the AGC investigator Caroll G. Donayre on Sept. 23, 2011 and put the lie to the fraud perpetrated by Watts and Norris in taking over the property in November of 2009.

"Mr. Kimball left the property and it was managed by another corporation. It was related to me that Mr. Kimball told the bank officials that he had tried to borrow more money but was unable to do so and that he had no money to pay the mortgage anymore. The December 30, 2009 and January 30, 2010 payments were not paid by the tenants and the loan was in default. The insurance policies had been cancelled and the county and state real estate taxes had not been paid. Maryland Bank & Trust Company, NA had received a notice of intent to file a mechanics lien on the property by a local contractor in the approximate amount of $200,000.00. Mr. Kimball asserts that I illegally foreclosed on his property. I believe my correspondence of February 4, 2010 clearly shows that my client had the right to foreclosure on the property. Marc Cohen, Esquire represented Mr. Kimball in the case. He replied in his correspondence of February 16, 2010 that he expected that the lessee, Maryland Bank & Trust Company NA, or its principals would make the mortgage payments. The lessee made two mortgage payments but the lessee could not pay the mortgage. Bank

officials relate that there was no agreement that the bank or any of its principals would pay the mortgage payments. I have seen no documentation of this alleged agreement. Certainly Mr. Cohen could have taken the necessary action to stop the foreclosure by either filing bankruptcy or filing a stay in the Circuit Court to resolve the default issues. This was not done and we proceeded with the foreclosure. After the foreclosure sale was finished Mr. Cohen and I resolved all issues. Mr. Kimball's attorney fees were paid, and the bank agreed to release any claim it may have had to the proceeds of the sale of the Kimball residence. The property was sold and Mrs. Kimball received all of the proceeds.

Mr. Kimball also provided that I was part of a criminal conspiracy to steal this property from his companies. Maryland Bank & Trust had almost $6,100,000.00 invested in this property. The last appraisal for the property, which was done in March of 2011, showed the appraised value was $3,445,000,00. Old Line Bank is now the owner of the property. The highest offer they have received for the property so far is less than $1,900,000.00. There has never been any possibility that anyone stole the property from him. The income from the lodge and restaurant has never been demonstrated that it could make any mortgage payment whatsoever while Mr. Kimball was the operator of the Lodge and Restaurant.

The Complainant and Mr. Cohen wanted Maryland Bank & Trust to pay Mr. Cohen's fees. (See January 12, 2010 letter from Marc Cohen to John Norris which is attached.) After the case was resolved I sent the check to Mr. Cohen. The idea that Mr. Cohen would not represent the Complainant's best interest in this case or that I would attempt to subvert his counsel is ridiculous."

Walter W. Sawyer III

THE FRAUD:

Walter W. Sawyer III, stated: *"The December 30, 2009 and January 30, 2010 payments were not paid by the tenants and the loan was in default."*

THE FACTS:

According to the Old Line Bank transaction records for the account listed in Charles & July Kimball's name for the loan on the property and obtained by Kimball in 2012, the following amounts were paid during the time that Sawyer asserted were not paid and which he based the foreclosure upon:

Nov. 23, 2009, $33,448.24

Dec. 23, 2009, $33, 248.24

Kimball also obtained a copy of the check used to pay the payment on Nov. 23, 2009. That check was signed by Bree Whitlock and made payable to Maryland Bank & Trust Co. with Kimball's mortgage loan account number referenced on the face of the check.

THE FRAUD:

Sawyer claimed that the mortgage payments were not made by the "lessees", who he knew was the bank, and that the bank had to make the payments. Sawyer claimed: *"The lessee made two mortgage payments but the lessee could not pay the mortgage."*

THE FACTS

The "lessee" was a sham corporation created by John B. Norris III and the restaurant and Lodge were run by Thomas B. Watts, the CEO of Maryland Bank & Trust and his designated manager, Bree Whitlock, who signed the November check making the mortgage payment.

IN a filing with the State of Maryland dated Nov. 4, 2009, John B. Norris III created the Limited Liability Company, Island Dining LLC and registered the firm with himself as the "Authorized Person" and also as the Resident Agent. From that day on, Norris was in a

KEN ROSSIGNOL

position to know who and what owned the stock in Island Dining LLC.

Watts told ST. MARY'S TODAY newspaper that the restaurant and bar were "packed" on New Year's Eve and that business was booming under the new management.

THE FRAUD

Sawyer stated that Kimball failed to pay a local contractor and that the contractor was placing a mechanics lien on the property.

THE FACTS

The money to pay the contractor was in Kimball's account but the bank failed to release the $177,392.18 due to AB&H Construction. The bank kept the money and never paid the contractor who had completed the work in June of 2009.

THE FRAUD

Sawyer asserted in his foreclosure letter and in the letter to the Maryland Attorney Grievance Commission that Kimball had failed to pay the real estate taxes, as justification for foreclosure.

THE FACTS

As of Sept. 30, 2011, the real estate taxes of $12,302.73 and $6,743.04 for the tax year July 1, 2011 to June 30, 2012 had yet to be paid and the tax bill was still being sent to Kimball. In 2012, the tax bill once again arrived in Kimball's mail.

THE FRAUD

Sawyer referred to "tenants" as being unable to make the mortgage payments, as being a company apart from the bank.

THE FACTS

It was clear to Sawyer that the Bank was operating the property in spite of his letter to Kimball announcing the foreclosure and his response to the Attorney

Grievance Commission. John Norris III provided a copy of an e-mail dated Dec. 30, 2009 from Marc Cohen:

"John: Bank sent Chuck for Island Hospitality LLC a RoomMaster license Transfer agreement transferring the software licensing rights to Bree as the facility's "new owner". I reviewed it and can suggest Chuck sign and send back to Bank if you advise me this is what is wanted. Also, did you get my invoice for services to date and were you able to forward it to Bank yet? Regards, Marc."

THE FRAUD

Sawyer prosecuted the foreclosure in spite of knowingly being a part of or in possession of facts surrounding the fraudulent lease which Kimball was forced to sign and the subsequent payments which were made on Kimball's loan account and the fact that the mortgage was not in arrears when he began foreclosure proceedings.

THE FACTS

Sawyer was personally enriched by conducting the foreclosure. He was paid a fee of $20,000 out of the proceeds of the sale of the Kimball property, according to the Auditor's Report prepared by Joseph Ernest Bell II.

Letter from John B. Norris III in response to Maryland Attorney Grievance Commission

On Sept. 30, 2011, John B. Norris III sent this letter to the AGC:

Dear Carroll G. Donayre:

Thank you for your letter of Sept. 15, 2011 regarding allegations of Charles Kimball. I would have responded sooner, but had closed my private practice in August of this year to accept the position of County Attorney for Calvert County. Therefore access my files regarding my representation of Maryland Bank & Trust

KEN ROSSIGNOL

Company in the transactions to which Mr. Kimball refers can only be had after work hours.

My response is not intended to disparage Mr. Kimball in any way. I truly believe that Mr. Kimball is mistaken in his recollection of whom he has spoken with and attributes the discussions he had with my client, before I became involved, to me. Upon commencing work with my client regarding Mr. Kimball's projected deficiencies, I learned that Mr. Kimball was represented by Marc Cohen, Esq. of Ober, Kaler, Grimes and Schriver. During the relevant time period, Mr. Kimball did call my office on numerous occasions and requested that I speak with him, though he was represented by counsel. My staff was instructed and, to my knowledge, did tell Mr. Kimball that I would not speak with him directly without written permission from Mr. Cohen authorizing me to do so. The one occasion I recall taking a call from Mr. Kimball, I believe had called numerous times that day and I thought it may not be related to this matter where I was representing and adverse party. Mr. Kimball, however, did want to discuss the matter where I was representing and adverse party. That brief call was documented the same day in the December 7, 2009 e-mail from myself to Marc Cohen , Esq., counsel for Mr. Kimball and a partner at Ober, Kaler, Grimes & Schriver with a principal office in Baltimore, Maryland and, I believe, a home office in St. Mary's County, Maryland. That email was submitted by Mr. Kimball with his complaint. The December 7, 2009 e-mail indicates I advised Mr. Kimball that I could not speak with him and would be in touch with his attorney, Marc Cohen. In contacting Mr. Cohen on December 7, 2009, I made him aware of the call and that I had prepared revisions to documents that he was welcome to review and also copied Mr. Kimball's son, "Bipper", in the event Mr. Cohen was no longer representing Mr. Kimball. The

Bank of Crooks & Criminals

December 10, 2009 e-mail, also included with Mr. Kimball's complaint, reflects that Mr. Cohen states "there is no time or retainer left for any longer negotiation." I have attached the following additional documents from my files for your information:

1. *December 1, 2009 e-mail to my client regarding changes to a Letter of Intent for Mr. Kimball's signature indicating my intention to share the revisions with Mr. Cohen as counsel to Mr. Kimball.*
2. *December 10, 2009 e-mail from myself to Marc Cohen, Esq., attorney for Mr. Kimball, regarding negotiation with Mr. Cohen of a Letter of Intent, indicating that Mr. Cohen had tracked his proposed changes, and repudiation of an earlier assignment of leases by Mr. Cohen's client, Mr. Kimball.;*
3. *December 30, 2009 e-mail from Marc Cohen regarding the transfer of software licensing to the operator succeeding Mr. Kimball's company; and*
4. *Invoices from Marc Cohen and his associates to Mr. Kimball's company Chesapeake Stafford Restaurant LLC reflecting Mr. Cohen and his firm's representation of Mr. Kimball from November 18, 2009 through December 20, 2009 and reflecting numerous calls and correspondence between Mr. Cohen and myself on behalf of our clients.*

Copies of all signed documents were provided to Mr. Kimball's attorney, though it is my recollection that they were available in January of 2010 but not picked up until March 2010. I have additional e-mails from my client containing attorney-client discussions and negotiations with him prior to my involvement. If you are aware of any means I can share these messages without losing the attorney-client privilege, I will be happy to provide them to you. Please recall that Mr. Kimball was not my client, he was Mr. Cohen's; the attorney-client privileged e-mails I am referring to originated from representative of Maryland Bank & Trust, my client, who is not a alleging any wrongdoing and has, thus, not waived the privilege. I presume and believe that Mr. Kimball's mistaken recollection is genuine and not attributable to any malice on his part.

John B. Norris, III

THE FRAUD:

Watts ordered Kimball to sign a blank lease in Norris's office. Norris claimed his actions were lawful.

THE FACTS:

Norris, using the threat of foreclosure, made Kimball comply with the order of Maryland Bank & Trust CEO Thomas B. Watts to Kimball to sign blank leases. Norris did this in direct violation of the instructions of Kimball's attorney Marc Cohen, who pointed out the transgression in a written document.

If the Bar Counsel in Maryland were competent, this would have been cause for Norris to be disciplined or perhaps disbarred. Maryland law specifies that all persons to a contract be listed, that the document be dated and copies given to all parties. This did not happen, Kimball has yet to see who was the lessee of his business and property as the documents were never furnished to him by Norris. Cohen repeatedly has stated that he told Norris not to let Kimball sign anything except the "License". Cohen should have reported Norris for this transgression to the AGC.

THE FRAUD

Norris attempted to force Kimball to sign an affidavit that created false facts regarding his relationship with Dr. Nwaneri, specifically, that he was an investor in Kimball's business.

THE FACTS

It is illegal to create false documents. Dr. Nwaneri has repeatedly loaned money to Kimball for his projects and has also acted as a purchaser of various properties from Kimball. Nwaneri and Kimball both agree that the doctor was not a partner or member of any of Kimball's companies.

Attorney Grievance Commission Denies Kimball Complaint on Sawyer; Finds No Wrongdoing

On October 4, 2011, Carroll G. Donayre, just four days after the letter was written by Norris, with barely any time for Norris's letter to actually hit Donayre's desk, Donayre sent the following to Kimball:

"Enclosed you will find a copy of a letter dated September 23, 2011 from Walter Sawyer, Esquire. This letter responds to our inquiry concerning your complaint.

The jurisdiction of this office is generally limited to reviewing conduct that may be in violation of the Maryland Rules of Professional Conduct, established for lawyers who practice in Maryland. I have considered your complaint and the attorney's response. I do not find a sufficient basis for this office to take further action. I am therefore constrained to close the file at this time. Thank you for bringing this matter to our attention."

Besides receiving and reviewing the letter from Sawyer in response to Kimball's complaint it is apparent that the AGC investigator did nothing to investigate the complaint. He simply took Sawyer's word for the fact that he was an honest guy.

KEN ROSSIGNOL

Attorney Grievance Commission Denies Kimball Complaint on Norris; Finds No Wrongdoing

Donayre replied to Kimball on Oct. 18, 2011 with an identical letter that he had sent regarding Sawyer proving that form letters for non-investigations save the time of bureaucrats.

"The jurisdiction of this office is generally limited to reviewing conduct that may be in violation of the Maryland Rules of Professional Conduct, established for lawyers who practice in Maryland. I have considered your complaint and the attorney's response. I do not find a sufficient basis for this office to take further action. I am therefore constrained to close the file at this time. Thank you for bringing this matter to our attention."

LETTER FROM KIMBALL TO ATTORNEY GRIEVANCE COMMISSION BAR COUNSEL GLENN GROSSMAN

When a staff investigator told Kimball there was nothing the AGC could do, Kimball appealed to the chief Bar Counsel for the AGC, Glenn Grossman.

"In that it is my contention that attorneys Walter Sawyer, John Norris and Marc Cohen all violated the standards of professional conduct in my matters. I respectfully request for you to go forward with an investigation and review the materials which I believe will show you that your office should take actions in this matter regarding these attorneys," wrote Kimball on March 1, 2012.

Grossman in a letter dated March 30, 2012, also turned Kimball down and refused to take any action against the three attorneys.

Bar Counsel Letter to Kimball: Will Take No Action

"Dear Mr. Kimball: I acknowledge receipt of your letter dated March 1, 2012, requesting review of the decision by Assistant Bar Counsel Caroll G. Donayre not

Bank of Crooks & Criminals

*to docket your complaints against the above listed
attorneys.*

*The complaint against your attorney, Marc Cohen,
Esquire, was closed at your request. On September 12,
2011, you contacted Ms. Donayre and stated that you
had listed Mr. Cohen on your complaint by mistake.*

*On April 7, 2009, you and your business,
Chesapeake Stafford Restaurants , LLC, borrowed
$6,022,000.00 from Maryland Bank & Trust Co., N.A.,
secured by the inventory and equipment of the River
Creek Lodge and Restaurant. In late 2009, you leased
the property to Island Dining LLC. The tenant apparently
made two payments on the loan. The lender claims that
two payments were not made and that you were in
default on the loan. Your counsel wrote to the lender's
attorney, Mr. Sawyer, on February 16, 2010, stating that
the bank was "owed no arrearages and has no basis to
foreclose".*

*You allege that the bank, together with its
attorneys, coerced you to sign a blank lease and formed
a "ghost corporation" owned by the bank to lease the
property and drive the loan into default and foreclosure.*

*The bank successfully foreclosed on the secured
property. You took no action to challenge the validity of
the foreclosure proceedings.*

*Mr. Sawyer explained that he did not begin
representing the bank until January 2010, after the
lease was signed and you allegedly failed to make the
payment due December 30, 2009. Mr. Sawyer's letter
dated February 4, 2010 described numerous defaults on
the loan.*

*Mr. Norris denies having discussions directly with
you concerning the loan or lease. He says that he
communicated with your counsel, Mr. Cohen. He also
provided copies of all signed documents to Mr. Cohen.*

KEN ROSSIGNOL

There is no evidence to establish that Mr. Sawyer and Mr. Norris were involved in a conspiracy to assist the bank in stealing the restaurant business from you. Since you borrowed six million dollars and the property is apparently now worth approximately two million dollars, there is no evidence that the bank profited from this transaction.

We will take no further action on your complaint.
Very truly yours,
Glenn M. Grossman
Bar Counsel

(**Author's Note**): The Bar Counsel clearly took no further action to investigate Mr. Kimball's allegations than to simply read the response letters from Norris and Sawyer and then pronounce the case closed, indicating that the staff of the office couldn't find a bleeding elephant in a snowstorm, at the risk of understanding the situation.

Kimball then sent a letter asking for help from Maryland Attorney Gen. Douglas Gansler, who cultivates an image of a hard-charging friend of the consumer who goes after big companies involved in all types of shenanigans.

Letter to Attorney General Gansler Asking for Help

Dear General Gansler:

I am writing to you today to request that your office open an investigation into the following matter.

"The CEO of Maryland Bank & Trust, Mr. Thomas B. Watts, created a straw company in 2009 that, under threat of foreclosure, he ordered me to lease my restaurant and hotel on St. George's Island, Maryland, to that straw company. Further, his attorney, John Norris, created the firm even though he knew it to be a fraudulent act and never provided either my attorney or myself a copy of the executed lease.

54

Bank of Crooks & Criminals

*"Within three months of Watts ordering me to sign
the lease, Watts then began foreclosure procedures
against me even though I had never failed to make a
payment as called for under the terms of my commercial
mortgage. While I never was able to see the name of
the person or firm that signed the lease I was forced to
sign, it is my belief and understanding that the bank was
that entity and the officers and attorneys of the bank
conspired to steal my property.*

*My property was taken from me in a fraudulent act
contrary of the laws of Maryland.*

*"I am a veteran of the United States Marines and a
have been involved in the construction and waterfront
development business for all of my life. I feel sure that
should you decide to investigate the facts of my case,
that you will agree that massive fraud involving my
bank and perhaps the successor bank with which
Maryland Bank merged, Old Line Bank, along with
actions of the attorneys involved, violated the laws of
Maryland and defrauded me of millions of dollars."*

The response from Gansler's office on March 30,
2012, was quick and decisive; telling Kimball that his
office doesn't handle such problems as a banker's
fraudulent acts cheating a person out of their property
and fortune.

*"Thank you for contacting the Maryland Office of
the Attorney General. I have been asked to respond to
your letter regarding your commercial transaction with
Maryland Bank & Trust.*

*"The Attorney General is the legal counsel for the
State of Maryland. As such, this office provides legal
advice to state agencies and investigates and
prosecutes crimes against the state. This Office does not
have authority to intervene in matters described in your
letter. I would suggest you consult with private counsel*

for advice and assistance in this matter. Peggie McKee, Citizen Response Coordinator."

Gansler is running hard to be Maryland's next Governor.

Both Thomas B. Watts and G. Thomas Daugherty are large contributors to political campaigns, mostly to Democrats. In 2010, Watts made a $1,000 donation to the campaign of Congressman Steny Hoyer, a sum typical of donations made by both men over the years to state and federal political campaigns. Campaign signs for U. S. Senator Ben Cardin were placed prominently on the property of Old Line Bank in the 2012 election. On July 31, 2012, Watts made a $2,500 donation to Hoyer's campaign. Tom B Watts (MD Bank and Trust/CEO), $1000 to HOYER FOR CONGRESS on 07/31/07.

July 15, 2005, Watts made a $1,000 donation to Hoyer's campaign. In 2004 election cycle, Watts donated a total of $2,500 to Hoyer's election effort. In 2001, Watts donated $1,000 to Hoyer's election campaign. In 1999, Watts gave Hoyer's campaign a donation of $500. Katie Watts, wife of Thomas Watts, gave $500 to HOYER FOR CONGRESS on 11/09/09.

In 2006, Helen Daugherty, wife of G. Thomas Daugherty, gave $1250 to the campaign of U. S. Senator Ben Cardin; G. THOMAS DAUGHERTY (SELF-EMPLOYED/ATTORNEY), $1250 to BEN CARDIN FOR SENATE on 06/30/06; Tom Daugherty (Maryland Bank and Trust Company NA/), $429 to AMERICAN BANKERS ASSOCIATION PAC (BANKPAC) on 02/18/09; G. Thomas Daugherty (Maryland Bank & Trust/President), gave $1000 to HOYER FOR CONGRESS on 07/16/10. G. Thomas Daugherty (Maryland Bank & Trust/President), $500 to HOYER FOR CONGRESS on 10/15/09. G. Thomas Daugherty (Maryland Bank & Trust/President), $1000 to HOYER FOR CONGRESS on 06/28/08. Thomas

Bank of Crooks & Criminals

Daugherty (Maryland Bank & Trust Co/Banker), $250 to HILLARY CLINTON FOR PRESIDENT on 02/08/08. Thomas Daugherty (Maryland Bank & Trust/President), $500 to HOYER FOR CONGRESS on 07/31/07. G. Thomas Daugherty (Maryland Bank & Trust/President), $900 to HOYER FOR CONGRESS on 04/10/06; G. Thomas Daugherty (Maryland Bank & Trust/President), G. Thomas Daugherty (Maryland Bank & Trust/President), $1000 to HOYER FOR CONGRESS on 07/09/05 LEXINGTON-PARK-MD. $1100 to HOYER FOR CONGRESS on 04/10/06; G. Thomas Daugherty (Self/Attorney), $500 to HOYER FOR CONGRESS on 07/23/02.

Marc Cohen donated $400.00 to Maryland Attorney General Doug Gansler's campaign committee, Friends of Doug Gansler, on 8/28/12 and another $1,200 on 10/2/12. Cohen also donated $500 on 10/27/11 to the Friends of Doug Gansler. The Daugherty LLC donated $100.00 to the Friends of Doug Gansler on 8/28/12.

Old Line and former Maryland Bank & Trust Board of Directors Member Frank E. Taylor gave Friends of Doug Gansler $1,000 on 8/20/12. Janet Bonaventure, who owns property in Baltimore, Maryland with Frank Bonaventure, of Ober/Kaler - and Frank Bonaventure is the attorney who billed Kimball for working on his case, and then was representing Old Line Bank when Kimball sought information – gave a $1,000.00 check to the Friends of Doug Gansler on 10/24/11, just six months before Attorney General Doug Gansler's office told Kimball that Gansler doesn't help consumers who have been defrauded by a bank. The Maryland Bank PAC gave Friends of Doug Gansler $500 on 7/19/12. Maryland Bank PAC donated $2,500 to Friends of Doug Gansler on 10/29/10. On 10/5/09 Frank Bonaventure donated $3,000 to Friends of Doug Gansler. The

57

KEN ROSSIGNOL
Maryland Bank PAC donated $2,000 to Friends of Doug
Gansler on 10/2/2009.

Bank of Crooks & Criminals

Kimball Becomes Stockholder in Old Line

After nearly a year of seeking a settlement from the bank, Kimball took the bull by the horns and bought twenty shares of stock in the bank. Then he contacted the bank's largest shareholder and chairman of the Board of Directors and told him what had taken place, and that Old Line Bank refused to give him the time of day.

For a while, at least, the bank was listening.

A bank vice president and two attorneys met with Kimball to hear his grievances, which is not the same thing as setting him straight financially. In September of 2011, Kimball met for hours with an Old Line attorney and gave a sworn deposition of the facts supporting his request to the bank to pay him $13 million, which, did not happen. To date, Kimball hasn't recovered a penny.

Kimball, not getting any satisfaction from the lower-level officials of Old Line Bank wrote directly to James W. Cornelsen, President and Chief Executive Officer.

This is the full text of Kimball's letter of April 18, 2012 to Cornelsen:

"On several occasions I have notified your bank of the fraudulent acts of Maryland Bank & Trust Company in relation to my property on St. George's Island, Maryland and the foreclosure which took place in 2010, thereby robbing me of all that I invested and the profits I may have made in the future.

"The response of your company to my many requests appear to be designed, not to be honest and forthcoming, but instead to delay and deny my requests for you, as honest businessmen, to correct the wrongs inflicted upon me and to make me whole. Instead, you simply have decided to leave me in the hole and cover

up the mess created by your bank officials and even your own attorneys.

"The acts of Mr. Thomas B. Watts and Maryland Bank & Trust Company are the acts of Old Line Bank. Two members of the board of directors of MBT are also now members of the board of directors of Old Line Bank, and one of them, George Daugherty, has invested $5 million in Old Line Bank. Mr. Watts was on your board for two months until you decided, for unknown reasons, to eliminate him as a director. When I notified your officers of fraudulent acts in the illegal foreclosure of my property, your executive refused to meet with me after first making an appointment with me. Your attorney told me I had no business with you, but I now have learned that your attorney was actually my attorney too, in an amazing conflict of interest. I have even bought stock in Old Line Bank in order to be able to have access to information about those who have stolen my money and my property.

"I have made myself available to your replacement attorney to provide documents and answers to his questions. Months have passed and it sure looks to me like you are betting this old Marine will kick the bucket and your problems and responsibilities will pass. That ain't going to happen. This is your last chance to make me whole. I suggest you provide an offer to me within ten business days of this letter that will rectify the fraudulent acts of your bank, the bank you bought (complete with assets and liabilities) and the acts of MBT and Old Line directors, as I will be looking for relief from the lot of you. I will be happy to sign any confidentiality agreement needed so the general public won't learn of the criminal acts which have taken place and committed by your various joint bank officials and attorneys."

Kimball says, "My bank intentionally put me into default and never made the payments as called for in the lease they told me to sign. They intentionally put me into foreclosure and did so fraudulently."

Only time will tell if Old Line sings a new song.

Kimball made repeated efforts as recently as the past several months to have Old Line take action to restore his financial condition. Kimball lacks the financial ability to employ a civil attorney.

Letter from Old Line Bank attorney Charles Henderson to Kimball

On Dec. 26, 2012, the new law firm for Old Line Bank sent Kimball a letter, signed by Charles H. Henderson, of the firm McNamee Hosea, Attorneys & Advisors:

Henderson wrote: *"I am in receipt of your unsolicited voicemail message of December 21, 2012, in which you request a meeting with James Cornelsen, the President and Chief Executive Officer of Old Line Bank, and me, prior to January 1, 2013. You have made multiple unsolicited phone calls to, and requests of, this office, which we have diligently responded to and attempted to accommodate on all prior instances. However, I am unable to arrange such a meeting at this time. If you have particular concerns, please outline those issues in a letter to me for consideration."*

Kimball is not the only small business owner to have bellied up in the current depression. But he may be one who can prove that his bank intentionally and fraudulently foreclosed on him, and when he attempted to warn the new bank buying his bank, they ignored him, even though one of their attorneys knew of the fraud.

Maryland Bank & Trust, aided by its attorneys, had become a criminal enterprise and gave every appearance of being nothing more than a sophisticated version of the mafia. John Norris recently became the county attorney for Calvert County after conducting a private practice for about six years following a stint as St. Mary's County attorney.

Norris's role in the criminal conspiracy to defraud Kimball included him actually drawing up the legal documents that formed the "ghost corporation" to whom he forced Kimball to sign over the property, which Sawyer referred to as the "tenant" but was nothing more than a shell corporation for Watts and Maryland Bank & Trust.

Norris filed the corporate charter approval with the State of Maryland on November 6, 2009 under the name Island Hospitality LLC.

Walter Sawyer continued in private practice up until the time of his death in 2012.

Sawyer never provided a default letter to Kimball until after the foreclosure had taken place, and had he lived, his complicity in the bank's fraudulent foreclosure, if proven, would have been revealed.

Marc Cohen is billed as the head of health litigation on his firm's website.

American Banker said this about Old Line acquiring Maryland Bank & Trust:

Maryland Bankcorp's credit problems are elevated, and that may well be reflected in the deal price. Old Line agreed to pay $30.93 a share, which works out to 80% of Maryland Bankcorp's tangible book. Though well capitalized as of June 30, 2009, Maryland Bank & Trust has been contending with some credit issues. At the end of the second quarter, noncurrent loans made up 5.17% of its total loans, an increase of 121 basis points from the end of 2009. That compares to an average of

4.33% for all Maryland commercial banks at the end of the second quarter. Old Line Bank's noncurrent loan ratio was 1.62% for the same period.

Watts and G. Thomas Daugherty, his brother in law, were given seats on the Board of Directors of Old Line Bank when the sale was completed.

The following information was taken from a filing on Form 8-K with the SEC from Old Line Bancshares Inc.

Pursuant to the Merger Agreement, on March 29, 2011, the Board of Directors of Bancshares and Old Line Bank appointed Thomas B. Watts, former Chairman and Chief Executive Officer of Maryland Bankcorp and G. Thomas Daugherty, former Chairman and Chief Executive Officer of Maryland Bankcorp, to their boards of directors. Bancshares' Board of Directors has not yet determined on which committees of the Board of Directors these individuals will serve. Messrs. Daugherty and Watts will receive the same compensation as currently paid to our other Board members-$400 for each Board of Directors meeting and a $2,000 quarterly retainer. As required by the merger agreement, Old Line Bank has entered into a three year non-compete agreement with Thomas B. Watts and G. Thomas Daugherty, in exchange for the sum of $200,000 payable to each in equal installments on a quarterly basis during the first two years of the term of such agreement.

According to Hotstocked.com, Christine Rush, the CFO of the Old Line Bank filed this notice with the SEC as required by the Securities Exchange Act of 1934:

On April 26, 2011, Thomas B. Watts resigned from the Board of Directors of Old Line Bancshares, Inc. (the "Company") and Old Line Bank, effective immediately. Mr. Watts did not resign in connection with any disagreement with the Company, the Bank or its management.

Why would Watts quit a position on the board of Old Line Bank just three weeks after the sale of the bank, which Old Line had billed as an "acquisition" and Maryland Bank had spun to the media as a "merger"?

Baltimore's *CityBizlist* reports the following:

George Thomas Daugherty, former president of Maryland Bancorp, has reported an 8.40 percent stake worth $5.22 million in Old Line Bancshares Inc. (Nasdaq CM: OLBK), the holding company for Old Line Bank. Daugherty, of Lexington Park, said he owned 575.084 shares in Old Line subsequent to last month's $21 million acquisition of Maryland Bancorp, the parent company of Maryland Bank & Trust Company N.A. The value is based on the stock's May 6 closing price of $9.07 per share.

And now Frank Taylor, a former director of Maryland Bank, has joined the Board of Old Line Bank.

Bloomberg Businessweek ran this article:

On July 21, 2011 the Board of Directors of Old Line Bancshares Inc. and its wholly owned subsidiary, Old Line Bank appointed Frank E. Taylor as a member of the Board of Directors of the company and Old Line Bank effective August 25, 2011. Mr. Taylor will be a member of the Asset and Liability Committee of the company and Old Line Bank.

Taylor, along with other directors of both banks, can be held personally liable for any criminal conduct that he knew about or should have known in his fiduciary role to the stockholders of the banks.

Taylor often played in a band known as "The Geezers" which also entertained at Kimball's Island Inn & Grill after the "tenant" seized the property from Kimball. At least one director of Maryland Bank had first-hand knowledge of the identity of the real operator of the restaurant and lodge. Or maybe Taylor was just one of the boys in the band.

Chapter Five

It is clear that Watts may have had a buyer for the Kimball property at St. George Island and then, perhaps, decided to steal it from Kimball in order to flip it and make a tidy profit; or he was trying to make the entire affair disappear. Whatever may have been in the works, it didn't work out. Old Line Bank now holds title to the property after purchasing Maryland Bank. Watts may have feared the bank examiners would look closely at a financial statement he, as the loan officer for Kimball, allegedly altered to induce a corresponding bank to pick up part of the loan.

THE FRAUD

Mysteriously, Kimball's financial net worth soared to $13 million dollars overnight, after Watts met with Kimball just before the loan was made to him for $6 million, according to sworn statements Kimball has provided in court proceedings.

How could Watts explain that Kimball's financial statement more than doubled overnight, just before he submitted the package to another bank to pick up part of the loan? How could Watts explain that to the bank examiners? That topic became a hot subject at depositions conducted in a lawsuit against Old Line Bank last year by Mrs. Nwaneri.

That was in April of 2009, and by November of 2009 Watts began the implementation of his scheme. As Sawyer laid out in his letter, the bank had no choice but to foreclose.

THE FACTS

Perhaps that is why they chose to ignore Kimball's financial backer, Dr. Nwaneri, who had the funds available and made it clear that those funds would be available to Kimball to help carry the place through the winter months and up to a year, if needed.. Dr.

Bank of Crooks & Criminals

Nwaneri, a prominent Washington physician, told me that he had already pledged properties worth over $1 million in order to borrow $1.6 million to add to the amount needed to finish the construction costs of the restaurant and lodge. He also said he put over a million dollars into certificates of deposit at the bank which he said he told Watts could be used to cover advances needed by Kimball over the coming year. Dr. Nwaneri has reiterated this information in three telephone calls and in a personal interview.

Just prior to foreclosing on Kimball, Watts told me that Dr. Nwaneri was tired of putting money into the operation. The doctor denies ever telling Watts that and, to the contrary, emphasized he was figuring to put up enough cash for ten months of the operation.

"I have had many long years of positive experience in loaning Chuck Kimball money, and I had no reason to stop," said the doctor. "He made me a lot of money for me over the years."

In an email to Watts on October 7, 2009, Dr. Nwaneri stated that he wanted to put up to one million dollars on deposit in Maryland Bank & Trust and said that he would allow the money to be used for Kimball's note payments.

"We can further discuss the possibility of the line of credit to further help the project," Dr. Nwaneri wrote to Watts.

Proving the claim of Dr. Nwaneri that he had the money available to pay the monthly payments for the Kimball property is a statement from Maryland Bank & Trust dated Nov. 2, 2009 which showed his previous balance as zero, his deposits as $457,171.98, zero withdrawals and interest paid of $1,339.46. A second account report of a different account number showed he had deposited an additional $660,389.53 on that date.

Evidently, Watts slipped in a surprise in documents he required Dr. Nwaneri to sign.

On November 9, 2009, following the deposit of over one million dollars into Maryland Bank & Trust, Dr. Nwaneri sent this email to Watts:

"Dear Mr. Watts, Following our meeting last Friday, I promised to get back to you by today or tomorrow. During our meeting you presented several documents for me to sign. Unfortunately, I signed the documents without any review or discussions with my attorneys (as stipulated in the documents). Perhaps you should have alerted me to that clause but you did not.

Mr. Kimball tells me that he has not been able to reach you despite your contention that it could not be so. There seems to be a lot of confusion.

I therefore hereby refer you to my attorney Bruce Marcus Esq. for all further communications. Please contact him urgently so all pertinent issues can be addressed and hopefully resolved. I will abide by any resolutions you arrive at with Mr. Marcus. Thank you."

Chapter Six

If Watts and Maryland Bank & Trust could force a default, which they did accomplish with their "ghost tenant," then they could move ahead with foreclosure on the River-Creek Lodge and Restaurant.

Kimball *never missed a payment* and was not behind on his loan and had access to more funds when Watts began to implement his scheme to defraud him of his restaurant and inn. Watts was successful. He got the property, he sold the bank, and Old Line Bank is now holding the bag.

In the six months from the time Watts gave Kimball a $6 million loan to supplement the $2 million Kimball had invested of his own funds, the issue of four waterfront lots owned by Dr. Nwaneri came into play. Watts and Norris had drawn up a document labeled "Affidavit of Charles S. Kimball", which was presented to Kimball in Norris's office when he signed the blank lease.

Kimball said he refused to sign this document, but during the deposition he gave, it was revealed that his signature had been affixed to the Affidavit.

The terms of the document were designed to show Dr. Nwaneri, not as a lender to Kimball's project but as an investor, who shared in the decision-making, in losses and in profits.

Thus Old Line Bank attorney Charles Henderson pushed Kimball hard during depositions to explain their business relationship and asked Kimball during a deposition held on Sept. 28, 2012:

"There are claims back and forth involving both Dr. Nwaneri and his spouse, Chinyere Nwaneri. Do you recall in the lawsuit that Dr. Nwaneri has alleged that you conspired with Old Line Bank to defraud him out of money?"

(Dr. Nwaneri's attorney Bruce Marcus objected)

Kimball: "I don't recall that, if it's in there, I don't recall that particular thing."

Henderson: "Sir, previously you testified that you did not recall the allegations made by Dr. Nwaneri in this case."

Kimball: "Is that the same question you asked me before regarding Dr. Nwaneri? I do not recall it."

Kimball has provided evidence of his assertion that Dr. Nwaneri routinely had given him power of attorney to sign any and all documents on his behalf in real estate transactions to buy and sell property, both general and specific. Besides the doctors hectic surgical schedule in the Washington area, he regularly flies to his native Nigeria where he donates his time performing operations.

Thus, over the past eighteen years there were many occasions when Kimball acted on behalf of Dr. Nwaneri.

The language in the document that Watts and Norris prepared attempted to put Dr. Nwaneri in the role of an investor in Kimball's business rather than the role he had played as a customer and a lender.

Kimball asserts that he never signed the Affidavit given to him by Watts and John Norris and the next day that Norris called and told him not to sign it.

After the bank foreclosed on Kimball's project the bank then moved to seize Dr. Nwaneri' s four waterfront lots and some commercial property in Washington, D.C..

At this point, Dr. Nwaneri's wife, Chinyere Nwaneri, became aware of the property having been posted as collateral for the loan to Kimball.

Mrs. Nwaneri only became aware of the foreclosure when the final papers ratifying the foreclosure were mailed to the Nwaneri residence.

Since her name was also on the properties but her signature wasn't, her concern developed into a lawsuit against the bank which has produced a public exposure of much of the information of the transactions, as well as a series of depositions of Watts and Kimball.

The issue of false certifications by a notary public to signatures may cause Old Line Bank to settle the case in Mrs. Nwaneri's favor.

Kimball says that Mrs. Nwaneri only became aware of the foreclosure when certified copies of the foreclosure were sent to her by the court auditor, J. Ernest Bell II.

During this process, Old Line apparently became aware of the conflict of interest issues, perhaps by listening to Kimball, and viewing the blizzard of documents that he routinely sent by express mail to the institution and to federal agencies that regulate banks; and Old Line obtained the services of McNamee Hosea.

According to those who have knowledge of the depositions, Watts appeared several times but cut short his appearance.

On one occasion, under questioning by Mrs. Nwaneri's attorney, Watts allegedly invoked his Fifth Amendment right to avoid incriminating himself and did so several times. At that point, the Old Line Bank attorney perhaps was concerned about Watts implicating Old Line Bank and advised him to stop his testimony and engage another attorney.

The next time Watts appeared, he was represented by a high-profile criminal defense attorney, William Brennan, who, according to legal sources, charges a minimum of $100,000 as a retainer. Brennan has been rated as one of the top 75 attorney's in the Washington metro area by *Washingtonian* magazine.

With the likelihood of the signature of Mrs. Nwaneri being forged, the possibility of a settlement of her lawsuit against the bank is very real.

What was the questioning where Watts pleaded the Fifth Amendment so as to not incriminate himself?

According to Dr. Nwaneri, who was present for the questions, his lawyer was questioning Watts about his relationship with his "attractive lady-friend", Bree Whitlock and her role as the manager installed by Watts as soon as he forced Kimball out of the River Creek Lodge and Restaurant.

Apparently, the legal ramifications for Watts, personally, as may be affected with his own marriage, the marriage of Whitlock, the operations of the bank and other unknown factors, could have been serious, legally, professionally and financially.

Kimball was questioned closely about his allegation that the financial statement completed by him on Kimball's behalf, to induce two federally-insured institutions to make loans to Kimball included a false statement as to the total value of the project.

Bruce Marcus, attorney for Dr. Nwaneri, asked Kimball:

"And where it says, market value for that lodge and restaurant, $13 million, who put that number in there?"

(At this point, the attorney for Old Line Bank, Charles Henderson, objected)

Kimball: "Mr. Watts."

Marcus: "Do you know – did you ever have a discussion with Mr. Watts where he ever told you that he thought the value of the property was $13 million?"

Kimball: "No, sir."

Marcus: "Did Mr. Watts, on your behalf, and Maryland Bank & Trust order appraisals of this property?"

Kimball: "They had, yes. Yes."

Marcus: "And so..."

Kimball: "Quite a few."

Marcus: "At the time Mr. Watts was putting $13 million on this financial statement, did he have an appraisal that showed $13 million?"

(Mr. Henderson objected)

Kimball: "They had four appraisals and they would not show them to me."

Marcus: "Okay."

Kimball: "Mr. Watts would not show those things to me."

Marcus: "Okay. Have you ever – did Mr. Watts ever tell you that he was aware that the property – or he believed that the property located in St. Mary's County (the hotel and restaurant) was worth $13 million?"

(Objection by Henderson)

Kimball: "Bruce, excuse me. What was that question again, I was looking at something.."

Marcus: "Let me restate it. Did Mr. Watts ever tell you that in his opinion, separate and apart from any appraisal, that the property was worth $13 million?"

Kimball: "No, sir."

Marcus: "Now can you tell me, sir, going down where it says, banks or finance companies where credit has been obtained, Maryland Bank & Trust, $4.4 million. Do you see that?"

Kimball: "Yes, sir."

Marcus: "Did you owe Maryland Bank & Trust $4.4 million? Was Mr. Watts aware that you had borrowed over $4 million from his bank as of 2008?"

(Objection by Henderson)

KEN ROSSIGNOL

Kimball: "He had to approve that."

Marcus: "Okay. And did you owe $4 million to the bank as of 2008?"

Kimball: "Yes, sir."

Marcus: "Did Mr. Watts ever tell you that there was a shortfall in the amount of money that you had borrowed with that which was necessary in order to complete the project?"

(Objection by Henderson)

Kimball: "No, sir. He didn't but one of the ladies in finance did. That's the letter right there. That letter came to me six – I think it was six working days after we closed. We closed on the 31st of December and I guess because of bank reasons and everything for taxes, they wanted to close it then. So we closed on the 31st. Then I got the letter, right off the bat, we got another –and that's why we had to go get the other money."

Kimball was asked by Bruce Marcus, attorney for Dr. Nwaneri, about the meeting he had with the attorney's for Old Line Bank.

Marcus: "Now when you went to this meeting with Mr. Schweitzer, did they show you these financial statements?

Kimball: "No, sir."

(Objection by Henderson)

Marcus: "Did they ask you about whether or not Mr. Watts had ever completed a financial statement on your behalf?

Kimball: "No, sir."

Marcus: "In the course of the interview that they had to determine the claim – that's what the purpose of the meeting was – did he ever ask you about whether or not Ms. Norris refused to complete a financial statement that was erroneous at the Mr. Watt's request?"

Bank of Crooks & Criminals

The session ended with Kimball continuing to explain that Watts had changed his financial statement to reflect a value higher than what he believed to be the actual and truthful figure.

Chapter Seven

Kimball had borrowed nearly $5 million, put about $2 million of his own money into the project and had borrowed about $2 million from Dr. Nwaneri. By the spring of 2010, barely 12 months after closing his loan on the River-Creek Lodge and Restaurant, Watts had seized control and installed Bree Whitlock as the manager. But prior to that, at Watt's urging, Kimball had employed her as the manager.

During depositions in the case between Mrs. Nwaneri and Old Line Bank, the attorney for Dr. Nwaneri questioned Kimball closely about Watts and Whitlock, who are followers of each other on the social website "*Pin interest*".

The questioning went to the heart of the matter as to the

Kimball told attorney Bruce Marcus, that Whitlock had "...seemed very, very sharp. And Tom asked us to hire her, which we did."

Marcus: "Tom asked you to hire this good-looking young woman he brought in?"

Kimball: "Yes."

Marcus: "And did she ultimately take over operations of that restaurant?"

Kimball: "Oh, yes."

Marcus: "And how was that –that Ms. Whitlock, Mr. Watt's good-looking lady friend, wound up taking over the restaurant?"

Kimball: "I had already fired her once, and then he brought her back again; I fired her another time.

Marcus: "Okay."

Kimball: "And then one day in Tom's office, it was in November – early November, Tom asked me to come in and says, I got a way we can go on this thing, really get sales going or whatever. I said fine."

Bank of Crooks & Criminals

Marcus: "So when was it that Mr. Watts began to give you advice on how to operate the restaurant?"

(Old Line Bank attorney Charles Henderson objects)

Kimball: Early – early November. And actually I've got the exact date. Early November. We went into his office in Lexington Park, my son, Bip, myself, and he also had John Norris there, the bank's attorney."

Marcus: "John Norris was the bank's attorney?"

Kimball: "Yes, sir. And Watt's."

Marcus: "And Mr. Watt's attorney?"

Kimball: "Oh, yes."

Marcus: "And Maryland Bank & Trust?"

Kimball: "Oh, yes."

Marcus: "And did there ever come a time when Mr. Norris did work for a company that you theoretically owned?"

(Henderson objected.)

Kimball: "If you look on that financial statement, you'll see where Mr. Watts paid Norris some funds out of my account and never said what it was for."

Marcus: "And which document was it that Mr. Norris – or shows that Mr. Norris got paid?"

Kimball: "It's on there somewhere."

Marcus: "All right. Can you tell me which document it might be?"

Kimball: "It's one of those."

Marcus: Let me hand that to you sir, just to make sure."

Kimball: "You know what, it shows up here, Page, there are a couple of pages missing. If you want, I will fax – I will fax that to you when I get back, I'm looking for it."

Marcus: "Do you know why it was that..."

Kimball: "I'll send that to you."

KEN ROSSIGNOL

Marcus: "What entities were formed in conjunction with the development of this project? What different entities were created?"

Kimball: "We just had Potomac Land Limited and the – our companies was Chesapeake Restaurants – and Chesapeake – I forget – you asked me that once. I can't remember. But anyway, we already had that in. When we went to Tom Watt's office and there he told me he wanted to get Bree back in there, that he had a – no. Wait. Before he got Bree on – Tom said, I got somebody; I want you to come in the office we'll work it out. What we'll do is set up an LLC as a – sales outfit and production outfit, whatever, and we'll do a separate LLC. They will give you a lease that will make –take care of the payments. And I think you got it right there. Now the whole thing is, who's going to make the money? Is Watts going to – funnel the money through their holding account at the bank, which at the time was $55 million. Tom Watts told me that.

(Kimball was shown Exhibit 41)

Marcus: "Okay. Let me show you – let me just show you Exhibit 41, and ask if you've ever heard of an entity called Island Dining LLC?"

Kimball: "Oh, yes."

Chapter Eight

Dr. Nwaneri had loaned Kimball nearly $2 million for the project and had deposited another $1.2 million in Maryland Bank & Trust with instructions to Watts to use those funds for making the payments for River Creek Lodge and Restaurant which would easily carry the new business for a year or more.

Asked if Watts ever told him that his money was at risk, Dr. Nwaneri, in an interview, said: "Never, if he had told me, I would have said to him that I already instructed him to pay the payments out of my account."

When did you learn about the foreclosure?

"Only after it was over."

Did you sign the papers for Watts to borrow the money for this loan?

"Yes, he brought them to the hospital where I was performing surgery and we went out to the waiting room. I signed and he told me to sign my wife's name as well, he said it was okay to sign my wife's name and I told him I had to review the documents with my attorneys and only later did I learn that the language in the documents provided troubling amounts for interest and it wasn't legal for me to sign my wife's name, but I trusted that the CEO of the bank was acting lawfully."

What would you do if you knew the project was going into foreclosure?

"There was no reason for it to do so as I had sufficient money on deposit to pay the payments which would have protected the funds I had already borrowed from the bank and loaned to Kimball. If needed, I would have arranged the funds to buy the loans from the bank and get away from them entirely, why not, I had already tied up over $3 million there, I am convinced that Watts simply wanted to steal the property."

Will Old Line Bank quickly settle with Kimball, will a federal investigation into banking practices by Maryland Bank & Trust end with criminal charges against those involved? Could what happened to Kimball and perhaps others, result in civil and or criminal liabilities for the members of the board of directors of both Maryland Bank and Old Line Bank?

Will lawyers end up being disbarred?

So much drama!

These 'suits' in the bank and the law firms don't realize this about Kimball.

Once a Marine, always a Marine and he ain't going to kick the bucket and let them all off the hook.

"Tell them, Kimball is going after all of them," said Kimball when he was read all the information in this book and agreed everything was accurate, to the best of his knowledge and represented an correct summary of the events.

The bankers and lawyers may be holding their breath and simply hoping that Kimball will drop dead.

In fact, Kimball admits he made a statement to his family that he wished he could just take some pills and go to sleep forever, following the foreclosure of his property by Watts. He and his wife went to his doctor who put him on an anti-depressant, which he still takes, and after one visit to the psychiatric evaluation unit at St. Mary's Hospital, Kimball decided that group therapy was not for him. But the stress took its toll on Kimball, leading to heart surgery later that year and emergency brain surgery after a brain hemorrhage. Kimball says his doctors say that stress was leading factor in all of his health problems.

Since the bank defrauded him of his property, Kimball has had heart surgery, brain surgery and

Bank of Crooks & Criminals

recently underwent back surgery. Kimball truly had his head examined and the surgeon, who kept his ticker working, even after the foreclosure, was none other than Dr. Nwaneri. The "Doc" as Kimball calls him, saved his life, and was smart enough to protect where he had his money at risk. Kimball, the six-million dollar man, is healthy and vows to never quit his efforts to be 'made whole' by the bank of crooks and criminals.

Editorial Opinion:

Were Thomas B. Watts and the Board of Directors really trying to protect the stockholders of the bank from a loss on a business to which it had extended a six million loan just six months before?

Wouldn't stockholders and bank regulators find it to be odd, or unusual, for a bank to lend such a large amount of money in the middle of a dramatic recession and then, before the business has a chance to succeed, pull the plug on it?

Were Thomas Watts and John B. Norris III criminally liable for creating a phantom corporation that they used to financially break Kimball, assuring that no other lender would step in, threatens Kimball with foreclosure and hold a gun to his head over losing his home as well unless he completely and totally adhered to the wishes of Watts?

Are the Boards of Directors for both Maryland Bank & Trust and Old Line Bank all responsible, both criminally and civilly for the actions of Watts?

If Watts were truly interested in safeguarding the loan the bank had made to Kimball, wouldn't it have made more sense to simply ask Dr. Nwaneri to take over the loans, knowing that he:

1. Had already borrowed nearly $2 million from the bank and loaned it to Kimball for the project and not only was willing to give Kimball more money but would have wanted to safeguard what he already had at risk.

2. Had already put more than $1 million on deposit with the bank and told Watts to use it for making payments as needed.

Watts knew how to reach the busy surgeon by phone but never advised him that he should step in to prevent the foreclosure.

Had Watts done the above, he wouldn't have been putting the loan at risk, perhaps explaining why the bank had been put under an enforcement action by the Comptroller of the Currency requiring the bank to acquire competent management.

It is my opinion that Watts simply was trying to steal the property from Kimball and the collateralized properties of Dr. Nwaneri as well.

Unless Old Line Bank or the law steps in, the *bank of crooks and criminals* has won.

Watts may not have achieved his entire scheme but he did get the property and was able to unload the bank which may have had a secret about his dirty dealings locked away in the vault.

About the Author:

After covering hard news for twenty-two years while publishing a weekly newspaper, Rossignol sold the newspaper in 2010 and has begun devoting full time to writing and is now the author of sixteen books.

As a maritime history speaker, Rossignol enjoys meeting audiences around the world and discussing the original news stories of the sinking of the RMS Titanic and other maritime history topics.

As of 2012, Rossignol has appeared on nine ships in the Pacific, Atlantic, and Caribbean discussing the stories of the heroes of the Titanic, the explorations of the new world voyagers, the Bermuda Triangle, and the history of piracy.

Rossignol appears at the Titanic Museum Attractions in Pigeon Forge, Tennessee, and Branson, Missouri, for book signings and to talk with visitors about the RMS Titanic.

He has appeared on Good Morning America, ABC 20/20; ABC World News Tonight and in a 2012 production of Discovery Channel Investigation Motives & Murders Series, "A Body in the Bay".

News coverage of Rossignol's landmark civil rights case, represented by Levine Sullivan Koch & Schulz re: United States Fourth Circuit Court of Appeals Rossignol v Voorhaar, 2003, included articles in most major news outlets, as well as a column by syndicated columnists James J. Kilpatrick.

The story of the St. Mary's Today newspaper is now available in e-book and paperback: The Story of THE RAG! The book includes nearly two hundred editorial cartoons that appeared over the years.

A strong highway safety advocate, Rossignol also publishes the DWIHitParade.com which focuses on impaired driving and the monthly publication, The Chesapeake.

News coverage of Rossignol's DWIHitParade won an Emmy in 2012 for WJLA reporter Jay Korff and coverage of the St. Mary's Today newspaper by WUSA reporter Bruce Leshan was awarded an Emmy in 2000.

Made in the USA
Lexington, KY
26 February 2013